The INDIAN REALITY

The INDIAN REALITY

CHANGING NARRATIVES, SHIFTING PERCEPTIONS

RAM MADHAV

RUPA

Published by
Rupa Publications India Pvt. Ltd 2024
7/16, Ansari Road, Daryaganj
New Delhi 110002

Sales centres:
Bengaluru Chenna Hyderabad
Jaipur Kathmandu Kolkata
Mumbai Prayagraj

P-ISBN: 978-81-969113-4-8
E-ISBN: 978-81-969113-2-4

First impression 2024

10 9 8 7 6 5 4 3 2 1

Printed in India

Contents

Good Governance

Home and the World

New Realities and Challenges

Preface

In 2020, a compilation of my articles written over the last five years was published in the form of a book titled, *Because India Comes First: Reflections on Nationalism, Identity and Culture.* By the time of its publication, the dreaded Covid-19 pandemic had struck, and the world had come to a grinding halt. India too braced up to tackle the challenge, and the ensuing two years witnessed gigantic governmental efforts, supported by inspiring popular will and activism that saw the nation of 1.4 billion scrape through the worst healthcare crisis, least bruised.

The Covid-19 pandemic played a catalyzing role, too, in the transformative changes occurring in the body politic of the global order in the twenty-first century. The new century brought new realities to mankind. The rise of China as a powerful force has led to tectonic shifts in the geostrategic landscape. On the other hand, the emergence of several states and minilaterals like India, Association of Southeast Asian Nations (ASEAN), Australia, South Africa, Brazil and European Union (EU) affirmed that the world has moved into multipolarity. Multilateralism of the last century, which evolved through bipolar Cold War years, became less and less relevant and influential for the world at large.

Multinational business corporations and digital tech giants, transnational non-governmental organizations, global terror outfits, universal religious and spiritual gurus and movements, and even some influential individuals like George Soros and

Bill Gates added a new dimension to the transition in the world. Many of them became so powerful as to defy national boundaries and the sovereign authority of the governments.

Cold War era issues of trade, economy and security took a backseat, yielding space to new agendas like environment, healthcare, Artificial Intelligence and robotics and a rights-focussed discourse influenced by woke narratives at the global stage.

Post-Covid-19 world is a completely new world. A new reality has overtaken countries and its population. It called for a new discourse and a new understanding of the reality.

In India too, the last decade witnessed tectonic transformation in almost every walk of national life. A new wave of enthusiasm engulfed the nation and a new pride overwhelmed Indians living across the world.

A significant milestone in India's twenty-first century trajectory was the return of Prime Minister (PM) Narendra Modi's government to power with an enhanced majority in the Parliament elections in 2019. The country trusted PM Modi's leadership in navigating through the transitional period in the history of the world and seized the opportunity that it was offering.

Under PM Modi's second term, India geared up to face the new reality. Its politics underwent a drastic transformation, from ruler-centric to people-centric. With his *Rashtra Sarvopari*–Nation First narrative, PM Modi had been able to unleash people's power massively during the onslaught of the Covid-19 pandemic. His efforts at making every last citizen of the country a stakeholder in its governance led to a woman from western Odisha (previously Orissa), a tribal region traditionally left behind, becoming the first citizen—President of India.

It is no exaggeration to state that almost everything in the country—its governance, politics, organizational culture—

is changing. The people too have changed. It is the New India rising.

In the last couple of years, I tried to capture the sense and essence of this emerging New India through my writings in various prestigious publications like *The Indian Express*, *Open Magazine*, *Hindustan Times*, *Malayala Manorama Magazine*, *India Today*, *The Print*, *The Daily Guardian*, *Swarajya*, *Organiser*, *India Foundation Journal* and *Chintan–India Foundation Blogs*. These articles covered aspects like how renewed efforts for building unity in the country are facing roadblocks, how the mainstream Hindutva movement is restating itself and how the people of the country, including its politicians, are having a relook at its history and learning.

I also wrote on issues of governance and international relations. India's journey in the last decade in these two areas—good governance and proactive foreign policy—will remain a topic for debate and study for many decades to come. While the country witnessed a decade of corruption-free governance with the economy making massive strides to place India at the fifth position in the world, country's politics continues to be plagued by acute acrimony and a new form of political untouchability.

However, on the foreign policy front, the country's rise has been spectacular. In no time, India catapulted itself from a reticent third world country to a frontline world power eager to rub shoulders with the mighty and powerful. A confident India is effectively standing up to secure its core national interests and tackle challenges on its borders and elsewhere, while at the same time donning the mantle of leadership in the neighbourhood, in Global South and in the world.

The Indian Reality: Changing Narratives, Shifting Perceptions presents my thoughts on all these issues. It is a compilation of my articles written over the last two years.

I am thankful to Rupa Publications for their interest in bringing out this compendium.

I hope the readers find it useful.

—Ram Madhav

President, India Foundation

New Delhi

AGENDA FOR LIVING TOGETHER

Samaano Mantrah Samitih Samaani
Samaanam Manas Saha-Chittamesham

May our prayers be one;
our brotherhood be one; our hearts be one.

—RIG VEDA 10.191.3

1

Droupadi Murmu, a President for Our Time

There is much to celebrate in the election of Droupadi Murmu as the fifteenth President of India in the *Amrit Mahotsav* year of Independence. In Murmu, the country not only has a Santhal tribal woman as the head of the state but also a leader from one of the country's poorest regions. Her rise from the tribal lands of western Odisha to become the first citizen of the country is a glowing tribute to the success of Indian democracy.

Murmu brings with her rich experience in public life. She is a well-educated woman from the family of a village headman. As a teacher, and later, as a people's representative—first as a councillor in the local municipal body and subsequently as a legislator and minister in the Odisha government—Murmu had brought development to a relatively backward region. She had also won the best performing legislator award.

Prime Minister Narendra Modi's knack for spotting people with unique credentials helped Murmu become the first woman governor of Jharkhand in 2015. Her tenure as the governor of an Opposition-led state was non-controversial, earning her the goodwill and support of the ruling party in the state, the Jharkhand Mukti Morcha (JMM), in the presidential election.

In India's constitutional history of seven decades, there

were a couple of occasions, mostly in the first couple of decades, when Presidents were elected unanimously. But if there was any other presidential contest that deserved consensus, it was Murmu's election. In any case, the odds were very much against the Opposition candidate, Yashwant Sinha. Had the Opposition demonstrated maturity and had Sinha withdrawn from the contest even at the last minute, especially after several of the Opposition parties including the JMM, Akali Dal and Shiv Sena extended support to Murmu's candidature, it would have not only enhanced the prestige of the Opposition but also helped to improve the political climate in the country.

We are living in an era of extreme political rivalry. We ended social untouchability in the country but have invented a new form of political untouchability. The days when a Vajpayee and a Nehru would praise each other, or a Vajpayee and a Narasimha Rao shared a healthy banter are fond memories now. At a town hall event during the 2008 US presidential election, when a Republican supporter made objectionable comments about Barack Obama, claiming that he was a Muslim and hence America was not safe in his hands, the Republican nominee, John McCain, interjected and categorically told him that Obama was a decent man and America would be absolutely safe in his hands. That kind of sagacity is missing in the political discourse globally now.

Unfortunately, the discourse during the run-up to the presidential election in India was vicious. Presidential elections were cordial and low-profile events in the past. In 1967, Zakir Husain was the presidential candidate from the ruling party. The Opposition had fielded Koka Subba Rao, a retired chief justice of India. There was no campaign from either side. In fact, Zakir Husain was at the Michigan University delivering the convocation address until three days before the election.

When asked about the campaign, Zakir saab quipped, 'We in India only stand, and do not run.'

But the presidential elections today are no less hectic and politically charged than the general elections. While Murmu maintained a dignified and low-profile campaign, the Opposition went ballistic from day one. Efforts were made to project the National Democratic Alliance candidate as someone who could not speak for herself—she was called a *murti* (statue)—and it was suggested that she would be a rubber stamp. If anything, it displayed the innate classist temperament that continues to prevail in some sections of our society.

In his final address to the Constituent Assembly on 26 November 1949, the chairman, Rajendra Prasad, who later became the first president of India, called this mindset 'sophisticated' when some members expressed doubts over the ability of Indian masses to use the right of franchise diligently. 'Some people have doubted the wisdom of adult franchise... In my opinion, our village people possess intelligence and common sense. They also have a culture which the sophisticated people of today may not appreciate, but which is solid,' he said.

It is another matter that the president of India is not equal in powers to the president of America although the same nomenclature was adopted. Both B.R. Ambedkar and Rajendra Prasad have clarified that it was more on the lines of the British monarch. Although the president is elected through an electoral college, he or she is a 'Constitutional President', Rajendra Prasad had explained.

All the presidents of India have understood the constitutional position and conducted themselves in office with great dignity and decorum. There were occasions when presidents had acted as per their conscience but never violated the constitutional limits imposed on them. Rajendra Prasad's famous correspondence with Nehru where he disagreed with several aspects of the Hindu Code Bill is a reference material for students of constitutional studies. Sadly, in the Opposition's criticism of Murmu, one finds the desire for a 'confrontational' President rather than a constitutional one.

Murmu's election will naturally make millions of tribal people of India happy and truly empowered. But the real success of our democracy is when she is looked at as not merely a 'tribal president' but the president of the 1.3 billion people-strong Republic of India. For her election to symbolize the bridging of the gap between the first and last citizens of our republic, people should celebrate the occasion by installing her picture in every public space.

2

An Agenda for Living Together

India is a land of extreme diversity—in language, social order, cuisine, customs and religion. Over millennia, it has mastered the art of managing that diversity and maintaining unity.

Samaano Mantrah Samitih Samaani
Samaanam Manas Saha-Chittamesham

This Rig Veda mantra laid down conditions for living together for the diverse Indian society. It means, 'May our prayers be one; our brotherhood be one; our hearts be one'. Here, the sages paused. They did not insist that 'our minds also be one'. Acknowledging the 'freedom of thought', they said—'May thinking minds be together'.

Traditionally, 'diversity of thought and unity of heart' has been the essence of Hindu civilizational philosophy. This catholicity allowed philosophical schools like Tarka and Mimansa—dialectics, reasoning, reflection and investigation—to flourish. Tolerance and acceptance became India's main attributes.

Across the planet, the Semites in Europe thought differently. There was only 'one truth' revealed by prophets, they insisted and called upon the followers to become 'believers'. Those who questioned became infidels and kafirs. Intolerance became the hallmark of the Semitic faiths.

The issue of 'living together' acquired complexity in India when these two world-views—one, exploratory and inclusive and the other, determinist and exclusive; one, that advocated 'seeking' and the other, that insisted on 'belief'—came face-to-face with each other.

Christianity and Islam, the two Semitic faiths, entered India and succeeded in converting a large number of Indians. The tolerant Indian milieu did not find it objectionable until a change of faith led to change of life for the converted. A new conflict was born when the neo-Semites started rejecting hoary principles of Indian ethos like *Sarv Panth Samaadar* (equal respect to all religions) and *Ekam Sat Viprah Bahudha Vadanti* (truth is one, wise men interpret it differently).

Islam's case is more intriguing. It came to India with the Islamic invader Mohammed bin Qasim in 712 CE. The next eight centuries saw waves of Arab, Turkish and Central Asian Muslim invaders attacking India. Although invasions across the Hindu Kush were not new, Islamic invasions differed from the earlier ones like Greeks, Huns, Sakas and Kushans. They brought medieval exclusivist, intolerant and iconoclastic Islam with them.

Will Durant, the American historian, called those conquests 'probably the bloodiest story in history'. They resulted in acute mistrust, disunity and animosity between Hindus and Muslims.

Al-Biruni, the Iranian scholar, who came to India with the invading armies of Mahmud Ghaznavi in the early eleventh century, pompously claimed that Islamic institutions were 'much superior' and all the customs and usages of local communities were known for their 'essential foulness'. He dismissed Hindus for 'their ludicrous views' and called them 'by nature niggardly…'. He also admitted that Ghaznavi's iconoclasm had led Hindus to 'cherish the most inveterate aversion toward all Muslims'.

Nearly three centuries later, Ibn Batuta, an explorer and traveller in the Islamic lands, observed that Hindus and Muslims lived in entirely separate communities. 'It is the custom among the heathen of the Malabar country that no Muslim should enter their houses or use their vessels for eating purposes. If a Muslim is fed out of their vessels, they either break the vessels or give them away to the Muslims,' Batuta wrote.

'Allah and Mohammad could not be accommodated in the Hindu pantheon,' quips eminent historiographer B.R. Nanda.

But there were phases of bonhomie too. Emperor Jahangir's mother was a Hindu. Jahangir's Hindu wife gave birth to his successor, Shah Jahan. Aurangzeb had a Hindu wife too. The last Mughal ruler, Bahadur Shah Zafar's mother Lal Bai was a Hindu. Mughal royals like Akbar and Dara Shikoh demonstrated syncretism occasionally. Akbar had set up an establishment at Fatehpur Sikri for translating Indian scriptures. He got the Mahabharata translated into Persian and called it Razmnama (Book of Wars). Dara Shikoh, Aurangzeb's brother, had the Bhagavad Gita translated into Persian. He composed a study of commonalities in Hinduism and Islam and called it 'The Mingling of the Two Oceans'.

Aurangzeb, though, did not demonstrate any façade of syncretism. His rule was one of the bloodiest chapters in Hindu–Muslim relations. British Orientalist Stanley Lane-Poole wrote:

> For the first time in their history, the Mughals beheld a rigid Muslim in their emperor – a Muslim as sternly repressible of himself as of his people around him; a king who was prepared to stake his throne for the sake of his faith. He must have been fully conscious of the dangerous path he was pursuing, and well aware against every Hindu

sentiment. Yet he chose this course and adhered to this with unbending resolve.

However, as the Mughal rule declined, rural Muslims started returning to their old Hindu practices. Poor Muslims, especially in provinces like Bengal, were as caste-ridden as their Hindu counterparts. They also used to worship Goddess Kali and participate in Durga Puja. The British census report of 1901 noted that the poor and uneducated Muslims used to consult astrologers, look for auspicious days to start work and prayed to Hindu deities for all sorts of personal problems. Muslim communities in the princely states of Rajasthan, like the Meos who were converted by sword's edge during Rajput-Mughal wars, used to even celebrate Hindu festivals like Diwali, Dussehra and Janmashtami.

In North India, a new and syncretic Islam, Sufism, also started taking root. This tradition accommodated many Hindu practices like tolerance, saint and *dargah* worship.

The last Mughal Emperor Bahadur Shah Zafar believed that Hinduism and Islam share the same essence and tried to restore Hindu–Muslim concord. He filled his court and army with a large number of Hindus. In his path-breaking work on the Indian Rebellion of 1857, called the *The Indian War of Independence*, V.D. Savarkar wrote in exuberant terms about Zafar's enthroning in 1837:

> So, in the truer sense, we said that the raising of Bahadur Shah to the throne of India was… the declaration that the long-standing war between the Hindu and the Mohammedan had ended, that tyranny had ceased, and that the people of the soil were once more free to choose their own monarch… Let, then, Hindus and Mohammedans send forth their hearty, conscientious, and

> most loyal homage to this elected or freely accepted Emperor of their native soil on the 11th of May 1857!

The Indian Rebellion of 1857 shook the British confidence. They realized that a potential opposition to their rule was building up in the unity of various sections of the Indian society. George William Forrest, a British educator and author of *A History of the Indian Mutiny*, warned the British that the message of the 1857 revolt was that Hindus, Muslims, Brahmins and Shudras could all come together unitedly against the Raj.

Viceroy Canning got a wily idea. 'As we must rule over 150 million of people by a handful of Englishmen, let us do it in the manner best calculated to leave them divided and to inspire them with the greatest possible awe of our power and with the least suspicion of our motives,' he advised his superiors in London. Thus was born the British strategy of *Divide et Impera* or Divide and Rule.

Meanwhile, a new revivalist movement, known as Wahhabism, took birth in the mid-eighteenth century in Arab lands. Started by a Sunni cleric and theologian Muhammad Ibn Abd al-Wahhab, this puritanical and exclusivist movement became a dominant stream in the Islamic world. Heft was added to it when the new ruler of Arabia, Muhammad bin Saud Al Muqrin, accorded the status of official religion to it in 1744. Petrodollars added further impetus in the twentieth century. From Palestine to Pakistan, this hard-line Wahhabism is leading to the rise of radicalism and fundamentalism among Muslims today.

Wahhabism came to influence Indian Islam also. Al-Wahhab's contemporary was a Delhi-based Islamic theologian called Shah Waliullah Dehlawi. He saw a big threat to Islam in the growing influence of Hindu customs and beliefs among the

Muslims and decided to 'purify' Indian Islam. He went to the extent of welcoming the invasion of India by the ruler of Afghanistan, Ahmad Shah Abdali.

Then came the Ahl-e-Hadith movement that started in Bhopal. This puritanical movement was also an attempt at negating the growing Hindu–Muslim proximity. These revisionist and exclusivist movements had finally succeeded in their mission when the Hindus and Muslims, who had fought together in 1857, ended up fighting against each other nine decades later in 1947.

Sir Syed Ahmad Khan, the founder of Aligarh Muslim University, was a classic example of the success of Wahhabi ideology in India. He started off as a strong protagonist of Hindu–Muslim unity. Addressing a large gathering in Gurdaspur in 1884, he exhorted: 'O Hindus and Muslims! Do you belong to a country other than India? Don't you live on the soil and are you not buried under it or cremated on its ghats? If you live and die on this land, then bear in mind that 'Hindu' and 'Muslim' is but religious word (sic): all the Hindus, Muslims and Christians who live in this country are one nation'.

But in a few years' time, the Wahhabists and the British had succeeded in transforming Syed into a rank fundamentalist. 'Oh, my brother Muslims! For seven hundred years in India, you had imperial sway. You know what it is to rule. The Bengalis had never at any period held sway over an inch of the Indian soil,' Syed exhorted a few years later. '...we do not want to become subjects of the Hindus instead of the subjects of the "People of the Book",' he proclaimed.

Syed Ahmed was one of the earliest Muslim leaders to propagate that Muslims were a separate entity. Hector Bolitho, author of *Jinnah, Creator of Pakistan*, described Syed as the first 'bold Indian Muslim' to talk about partition.

The next to champion this 'two-nation theory' was

Muhammad Ali Jinnah. Interestingly, Jinnah too started his political career as a champion of Hindu–Muslim unity. Indian political leader and social reformer Gopal Krishna Gokhale described Jinnah in 1910 as the 'Ambassador of Hindu–Muslim unity'. Jinnah was opposed to partition of Bengal in 1906 and worked for Hindu–Muslim unity until 1916. He told his Muslim citizens that the propaganda about Hindu domination was just 'a bogey, put before you by your enemies to frighten you'. But he turned into the champion of Muslim politics by 1936. In just two decades, from 'Hindu–Muslim unity', Jinnah flipped to 'Hindus and Muslims cannot live together'. From a leader decrying separate electorates in 1908, he transformed into a leader championing a separate nation for Muslims three decades later.

The two-nation theory of Jinnah was a fragile and lacklustre one. Intellectually, it was hollow and far removed from objective reality. Jinnah's argument that India's Muslims had a common identity was a facile one. Muslims lived all across India. They spoke different languages and followed different customs, often local and identical to Hindus. That's why Gandhi repeatedly told Jinnah and Muslims that there could not be any other homeland for them except India.

The fallacy of the two-nation theory was established on the day India was partitioned. Just about half of the Muslim population went over to Pakistan, while the rest remained in India, either out of compulsion—they could not afford a migration, or out of choice—they did not support partition. In just two decades time, the much-touted two-nation theory returned to haunt Pakistan when the Bengali-speaking Muslims wanted their own homeland and secured Bangladesh in 1971.

In Pakistan's Constituent Assembly in August 1947, Jinnah tried to please his Western masters by promising to build a secular country where the minorities would enjoy equal rights as the majority. But Pakistan became a quintessential theocracy. Jinnah knew well that there was nothing else that could keep the country together except Islam. To that was added 'hate India'. The country that Jinnah created out of the two-nation theory can only survive by promoting theocracy and hating India.

Division of India was not just about lands, but hearts too. Although Hindus and Muslims continued to live together in India after Partition, their hearts never met. The Hindu suspicion got fortified over decades due to Muslim intransigence on one hand and appeasement politics on the other. Kashmir and communal riots have fuelled this suspicion further.

Coming together requires this suspicion to end. It calls for attitudinal change. Unfortunately, large sections of Indian Islam continue to be influenced by Wahhabism. Indian Muslims must reject this exclusivist and hard-line version for a more inclusive, liberal and humanitarian Islam championed by institutions like Nahdlatul Ulama (NU) in Indonesia. The NU rejects the Saudi-sponsored Wahhabism. It declared that there were 'no kafirs'. It called for respect to all religions and dismissed the Islamist propaganda about 'Islamophobia' as a figment of imagination, if not the result of their own actions. It theologically held patriotism above *ummah* (community).

For greater national cohesion, Muslims in India should turn to the NU's approach. They should give up medieval concepts like blasphemy. Murders and murder threats in the name of blasphemy have seriously dented Hindu goodwill for Muslims. Many Hindus today believe that Muslims will not change.

On their part, Hindus too need to understand that perpetual hatred for Muslims cannot be the way forward. They cannot be angry at a stand-up comedian for insulting Hindu gods, and also demand the right to insult the prophet.

Theologies can be contested, but narratives about gods and prophets need to be viewed from a culture-specific lens. Every religion has narratives that others may find illogical.

As M.S. Golwalkar in 1948 and Mohan Bhagwat in 2018 reiterated, Hindu Rashtra does not exclude Muslims. A misplaced argument that Hindus cannot live with Muslims makes Jinnah happy in his grave while Gandhi and Golwalkar will squirm in theirs. There is a global demand that Islam should change. Hindus should demonstrate courage to help Muslims reform. They should handhold those Muslims who are fighting for that.

Continuous reform and upgradation are the unique virtues of Hindus. For Christianity, it took nearly 1,500 years, until Martin Luther came forward to challenge the orthodoxy, to reform. Islam is passing through its fifteenth century. Will a Muslim version of Luther surface? It is an important question for India.

Hindus are united and strong today. A serious dilemma haunts them. If the Muslim leadership fails to rise-up to the occasion, can this unity expand to encompass them? Or forced to fight back radical Islamist elements, will it end up creating a Semitic version of Hinduism—intolerant, xenophobic and aggressive?

Reprinted from INDIA FOUNDATION JOURNAL, with permission of India Foundation.

3

Why India's Minority Groups Are Not in Danger

India's first citizen is an 'Adivasi' woman from one of the remotest tribal areas in eastern India who succeeded a 'Dalit' President. Muslims, Christians and other 'minorities' hold high positions in government, judiciary and bureaucracy, and are Members of Parliament and legislators in states in large numbers. India's Sikh majority state of Punjab has a Sikh chief minister (CM). Christian majority states like Nagaland, Mizoram and Meghalaya have Christian CMs, some in alliance with the Bharatiya Janata Party (BJP). The minority welfare ministries across the country, including Uttar Pradesh with over 40 million Muslims[1], are in the hands of Muslim ministers.

In fact, in the last few years, systematic efforts by central and state governments have helped the poor and more discriminated sections within the Muslim community—the Pasmandas and Arzal—to rise in economic, social and political status in the country. Muslim women are the beneficiaries of measures regulating 'triple talaq', a regressive practice continuing in India even as most Islamic countries have rejected it.

With sporadic incidents involving individual members of different communities, India has been largely free of communal

[1]'C-01: Population by religious community, India – 2011', *censusindia.gov.in*, http://tinyurl.com/bdfh2hau. Accessed on 22 January 2024.

clashes in the last eight years, a regular occurrence across the country in the past. Even the reprehensible incidents of mob lynching were few and not limited to any one community. If there were Muslim victims, there were Hindu victims too. India's law and order establishment takes swift action against all culprits.

Yet, a paid advertisement in a prestigious American daily claimed that in India 'millions of citizens face religious persecution, discrimination and deadly mob violence'. The advertisement, released on the occasion of Mahatma Gandhi's birthday, goes against the central tenet of Gandhism—truth. It is filled with lies and innuendos, and there is no substantiation by facts or data. The concerned newspaper has categorized those blatant lies as an 'advertisement', but it should probably be called an 'advertorial'.

A simple fact-check would have prevented the prestigious newspaper from publishing this malice-filled piece.The criminal justice system in India and the law and order machinery are controlled by the governments of the Indian states, many of the larger ones controlled by the Opposition. Similarly, India's judiciary is highly reputed for its independent thinking and jurisprudence. Yet the propagandists peddle lies that 'Indian judiciary and police are filled with BJP/RSS loyalists'.

The global audience is constantly fed such misinformation, largely by groups inimical to India's democracy and interests. Pakistan-sponsored or Khalistan-inspired groups are conspicuous by their presence. But what lends credibility to such lies is the insidious lending of support by the left-liberal cabal in the West. Salvatore Babones, a respected Australian political sociologist, called these Western think tank elites the 'true barbarians'. Unable to accept the rejection of their biases by mainstream Indian society, these groups have now shifted their base to the Western world and are continuing their propaganda by firing from the shoulders of groups such as the ones that paid for the advertisement.

Such propaganda, although a public relations challenge for Indian embassies abroad, may not have any impact on average Indians. But the gullible among sections of the minority community may still fall for it, especially when sections of India's own political establishment, for their own political ends, seek to lend credibility to such a narrative.

Mallikarjun Kharge, the senior Congress leader and the president of the party, has 'warned' his partymen that if Prime Minister Modi gets strengthened further, 'the rule of *sanatan dharma* and RSS will come in this country'. From 'Hindutva forces', the Opposition leadership has now gone on to besmirch Sanatana Dharma. Kharge probably does not know that Gandhi always called himself a 'sanatani Hindu'. Jawaharlal Nehru wrote in *The Discovery of India* that 'Sanatana dharma, meaning the ancient religion, could be applied to any of the ancient Indian faiths (including Buddhism and Jainism)'.

It is a test for the ability of the minorities in general and Muslims in particular to see through the deviousness of this propaganda. There has always been a vested interest in creating the narrative of 'minorities in danger'. It was Jinnah who used it to the hilt before Partition. It has now become bread and butter for many liberals. The newly emerging Muslim leadership in the country should reject this cacophony and seize an opportunity that is being offered.

A large number of Muslim leaders have seen in the RSS an adversary all these years despite its engagement with the community right from the time of Guruji Golwalkar. Today, there is a thaw in the relations between the two. Some prominent members of the Muslim civil society have initiated a dialogue with the RSS chief recently, which was followed up by him visiting a madrasa in Delhi.

Bhagwat has been showing considerable openness in engaging with the Muslim community for quite some time now. His predecessors like Balasaheb Deoras, Rajendra Singh and Sudarshan also did it. This time, Bhagwat's efforts are more focussed. At a Muslim congregation once, he told the audience that they were not separate from the Hindu community. In his annual *Vijayadashami* address, the RSS chief told the audience that '*shakti shanti ke liye*' or strength should be for peace.

India is a large country. Its diversity is mind-boggling. It has centuries-old history of communal strife too. The Partition on communal lines was the singularly most harmful political development in the last century that had created a huge gulf between the two communities. The legacy of that communal strife manifests in occasional and sporadic flare ups. Yet, Indian society has always firmly kept up the ethos of 'unity in diversity'. It did not allow India to be converted into another version of Pakistan.

Managing 'diverse democracies' and preventing them from falling apart is seen as a big challenge by the Western world today. Yascha Mounk of Washington's Council on Foreign Relations called it 'the great experiment'. But in India, it was not merely an experiment; it has been the lived experience.

4

Hindu-Muslim Unity: A Lofty Ideal

While Hindus, Muslims and Christians reaffirm their commitment to tolerance and religious freedom, the majority still prefer to confine their relations in marriage and friendship to their co-religionists only.

In an engaging study on the religious-political reality of America, renowned journalists John Micklethwait and Adrian Wooldridge concluded in their book *The Right Nation: Conservative Power in America* that the more than two-century-old democracy has decisively shifted to the right. Religious and political conservatism has come to stay as the mainstream American identity for a long time to come, in spite of the Democratic Party intermittently coming to power, they opined.

A survey report released by the Washington-based Pew Research Centre on religion in India highlights similar interesting insights. Unlike America, India has a national history of several millennia. Its societal mores have evolved over a long and often intriguing historical journey. A politically, linguistically and socially diverse demography has been woven into a united society on the strength of an overarching religious-cultural identity. Swami Vivekananda had described this phenomenon in the words: '*Dharma Praana Bharata*', meaning the religious-cultural identity is the lifeline of India.

The Pew Research Centre's survey puts an affirmative seal on this description of India. India is a country of believers in God, a vast majority of whom were absolutely sure about god's existence. If the Buddhists, for whom belief in god was not a core tenet of religion, are excluded, almost 95 per cent of Indians of all other religions believe in God.[2] Most Indians, cutting across religions, also believe in extramundane concepts like karma, fate, reincarnation, purification and angels. That makes India the most religious country.

But then, the survey also underscores simmering contradictions among religions underneath this macro picture of religiosity. While Hindus, Muslims and Christians reaffirm their commitment to tolerance and religious freedom, the majority still prefer to confine their relations in marriage and friendship to their co-religionists only. Over 66 per cent Hindus said that they would prevent their men and women from marrying into other religions. This figure is even higher among the Muslims, 80 per cent of whom insisted that it was very important to stop their women from marrying outside the religion. Dietary habits like eating beef also divide the communities with over 72 per cent Hindus insisting that beef-eating was un-Hindu.[3] Although most great leaders of India's independence movement were opposed to India's partition, seven decades later, an increasing number of Hindus came to believe that Partition was good for the country.

Many of these findings of the Pew Research Centre's survey might not be great revelations for Indians. Despite occasional expression of sentiments about common DNA, a gulf existed between the major religious communities like

---

[2]Sahgal, Neha, et al., 'Religion in India: Tolerance and Segregation', *Pew Research Center*, 29 June 2021, http://tinyurl.com/25s7akds. Accessed on 26 December 2023.

[3]Ibid.

Hindus and Muslims over centuries. Seeds of this gulf were laid in what historian Will Durant described as 'probably the bloodiest story in history', namely the Islamic conquest of India. Efforts by Mughal Emperors like Akbar for syncretism did not succeed due to various historical factors like continued iconoclasm and religious orthodoxy under him and after. In any case, his successor Aurangzeb epitomized religious intolerance and bigotry. The British era had accentuated the divisions in the later centuries.

The revolt in 1857 was one occasion when the Hindu and Muslim sepoys came together to fight against the British. Cynics refuse to see it as a unity of minds insisting that the two had revolted for separate reasons—Hindus on the suspicion that the cartridges of the Enfield rifles, which required the sepoys to use their teeth to rip open, were greased with cow fat, while Muslims believed that pig fat was used for the same. Hindu sepoys swore by the waters of sacred Ganges while Muslim sepoys chose the holy Quran.

Yet, a staunch Hindutva ideologue like Savarkar had exuberantly called it a golden episode of Hindu-Muslim unity. Referring to the revolt in Delhi in May 1857, Savarkar wrote in *The Indian War of Independence*, '…these five days proclaimed by beat of drum the end of the continuous fight between the Hindus and the Mahomedans dating from the invasion of Mahmud of Ghazni and on these days it was proclaimed first that the Hindus and the Mahomedans are not rivals, not conquerors and conquered, but brethren. Bharat mata pronounced the sacred spell of these days. "Hence forward you are equal and brothers. I am equally the mother of you both."'

This exuberance remained short-lived. The rise of Muslim politics from Sir Syed Ahmad Khan to Muhammad Ali Jinnah had buried the hope for unity. Henceforth, Hindu–Muslim unity became a political obsession, with the objective of preventing the partition of the country. Gandhi was in the forefront pleading with the Muslims to remember that 'many Hindus and Mahomedans own the same ancestors and the same blood runs through their veins'. Nehru passionately told the students of Aligarh Muslim University in 1948, 'You are Muslim and I am a Hindu. But that does not take us away from that cultural inheritance that is yours as well as mine.'

Many leaders like Lala Lajpat Rai wanted Hindus and Muslims to come together, but were unsure given 'the injunctions of the Koran and Hadis'. Rai had hoped that the 'learned mind and wise head' of the Muslims would find a solution. Some, like B.R. Ambedkar, were however, dismissive of the idea. 'Before the Hindus complain of the destruction of the unity of India, let them make certain that the unity they are harping upon does exist. What unity is there between Pakistan and Hindustan?' wrote Ambedkar. In his opinion, the two communities were living in an armed truce only.

Seven decades after the Independence, as the Pew Research Centre's survey had shown, Hindu assertion has come to occupy the national centre stage in India with 65 per cent Hindus believing that Hindus and Indians were coterminous. Politics too did not help take Hindu–Muslim unity beyond a political strategy. Eminent psychologist Sudhir Kakkar grimly summed up the reality about inter-communal relations, saying: 'It was a multicultural coexistence rather than any merger into a single, composite culture. Hindus and Muslims lived together separately. They were more than strangers, not often enemies, but less than friends.'

It underscores the need for continued efforts for Hindu–Muslim unity. Those efforts should be viewed as a genuine and optimistic urge for building greater national cohesion.

Courtesy: India Today Digital.

5

A Nation-First Narrative

In the 1980s, Deng Xiaoping, the then supreme leader of the Chinese Communist Party, decided to focus exclusively on economic development. He realized that for the China dream to come true, the economy, shattered by Mao's decades of defective policies, must be reinvigorated.

The decade saw rapid economic growth and infrastructure development in the country. Foreign investors and technologies were invited to China. When his own colleagues in the party protested, accusing him of promoting capitalist policies, Deng shut them off with the retort that he did not care about 'the colour of the cat as long as it is catching the mice'. This ruthless pragmatism, and the courage to set ideologies aside for the larger national good, has helped China reach where it is today.

The developing world is now debating these issues. As James Carville, the campaign strategist for Bill Clinton, quipped in 1992—'It's the economy, stupid'. Countries are catching on to Carville's economic mantra, sidestepping ideological hamstrings. Whoever visited the Saudi Arabia pavilion at the Expo 2020 Dubai will vouch for the progressive and ultramodern presentation of the mothership of orthodox Islam. Live images of surging race cars with Saudi women at the wheels left every visitor fascinated and flabbergasted. The same is the case with countries in Asia and Africa.

But sadly, here we are, debating about communal polarization. Leaders of the Opposition are writing op-eds as if at every street corner in India, Hindus and Muslims have crossed swords. It may suit the political narrative for some, but it will certainly hurt the country's global narrative at a time when the leadership is steadfastly pursuing an agenda of growth and prosperity for every Indian. No other leadership appreciates this imperative better than the present one. The 2020s will be to India what the 1980s were to China. A decade of single-minded focus on the economy could unleash the country's latent potential and catapult it into the club of developed nations.

Pundits pointing fingers at the central government or some Hindu organization for this perceived polarization have a sinister agenda—they want to divert the national discourse by dragging the prime minister's name into it. But the actions of the government speak for its inclusive and a development-for-all approach.

Communalism will hurt India's prospects, but the exaggerated portrayal of it will hurt us more. Is the 1.3 billion-strong Indian society really polarized? Should some fringe elements be elevated to the status of 'makers of the national narrative' for a vast country like ours? Isn't it tantamount, for instance, to call the entire American society racist just because some truly reprehensible incidents of racial violence happened there?

India's communal problem is centuries old and it continues to erupt occasionally. This may be a kind of whataboutery, but isn't it hubristic on the part of some political leaders to pretentiously argue and take the moral high ground when their own cupboards are filled with horrific skeletons from communal orgies?

This is not to undermine the potential threat that communal

elements pose to India's national fabric. We paid a heavy price for it at the time of Independence. These elements, be it Muslim or Hindu, do not and should not represent our respective mainstream communities. To merely shrug off responsibility for their actions also amount to being communal apologists. There is a need to frame a civil society response to it.

Social media is partly to blame. It is democratic not only in nature and spirit but also in noise and chaos. Perceived injustices as portrayed on X (formerly Twitter) or Facebook impact sensible people too. But the problem is that different stories and images circulate among different recipient groups, making each believe that their religion is under attack from the other. While the image of an attack on a Hindu procession gets wider traction among Hindu user groups, similar provocative images of acts against a mosque or a Muslim group make their way to Muslim user groups. Hence, the important lesson is that the social media narrative needs to be viewed with greater equanimity and objectivity and that it allows the law-and-order establishment to take necessary action against the culprits.

These incidents are not all fictitious either. Every hate speech will have a fallout; every rape threat actually translates into a real incident. Hence, the social leadership should immediately come forward, condemn and explicitly state that such words and acts have no place in a civilized discourse.

Post-Independence India witnessed the pampering of minority communal politics for vote bank considerations by the same parties that are preaching morals today. Communalism begets communalism. That brand of politics of appeasement has ended for good in the country, so the Opposition is calling the new order majoritarian politics. The minority leadership should reconcile to their new status and end such minority-majority distinctions. Learning to live in harmony with the rest of our mainstream national society should be viewed as an important obligation.

It is also important that the Muslim leadership come out of the Wahhabist hard-line interpretations of Islam that seek to pit Muslims against non-Muslims and promote separatism and exclusivity. The return of debates focussed on hijab and niqab is symptomatic of this as also the rise of violent, ultra-radical outfits like the Popular Front of India. The solution to separatism lies in humanitarian Islam promoted by organizations like Nahdlatul Ulama under its chairman Yahya Cholil Staquf (also known as Pak Yahya). Nahdlatul Ulama's interpretation of Islam is the ideal model for the Islamic world to emulate.

The reaction of sections of Hindus, including some wearing saffron robes, is also utterly un-Hindu. Violent language and talk of annihilation of an entire community smack of their attempt at semitization of Hinduism. It is pertinent to note that mainstream Hindu organizations like the RSS have distanced themselves and disapproved of such rants.

Talk of polarization may be premature but the Indian social leadership needs to stand up to the forces of hatred and violence by invoking peace, inclusivity and a nation-first narrative. India's narrative of the decade should be 'it's the economy, stupid!' The onus lies on all of us.

Courtesy: India Today Magazine.

CONTEMPORARY HINDUTVA

'Hindutva is one that takes everyone along, brings everyone together, unites everyone within itself, and makes everyone prosper.'[4]

—DR MOHAN BHAGWAT
SARSANGHCHALAK (RASHTRIYA SWAYAMSEVAK SANGH)

[4]PTI, 'Hindutva Takes Everyone Along: Bhagwat', *The Week*, 29 September 2021, http://tinyurl.com/ycyythxd. Accessed on 26 December 2023.

6

Bhagwat's Bharat

Eminent American author Walter Andersen had once quipped that 'the RSS is difficult to understand and easy to misunderstand'. This misunderstanding stems mostly from deliberate misrepresentation of facts, but also sometimes because of the lack of articulation from the RSS (Rashtriya Swayamsevak Sangh). In the present case, since the interview was long and in Hindi, most commentators did not bother to read it fully. On its part, the *Panchjanya*, a weekly magazine published by the RSS, should have released an English transcript simultaneously for the benefit of those who wanted to understand the views of the head of the most influential organization today.

The RSS is not a fossilized body. It has constantly evolved with changing times. After independence, M.S. Golwalkar, the then chief of RSS, introduced several dimensions to the functioning of what is today described as the 'Sangh Parivar'. Balasaheb Deoras, Rajendra Singh, K.S. Sudarshan and later chiefs, too, introduced transformative changes in the functioning of the organization.

Mohan Bhagwat, the incumbent sarsanghchalak, is taking that transformation to the next level with greater openness. From a media-shy and introverted organization, the RSS has today emerged as the most visible force ready to engage with the world on all the contemporary issues and challenges.

Bhagwat has spoken candidly, even on issues like LGBTQ. Over the next few years, the RSS had firmed up its views on the issue and the Sarkaryavah (general secretary) of the organization, Dattatreya Hosabale, stated in a media interaction in 2016: 'I don't think homosexuality should be considered a criminal offence.' Two years later, in 2018, the Supreme Court struck down Section 377 of the Indian Penal Code, thus decriminalizing homosexuality.

In an interview, Bhagwat described homosexuality as 'biological' and said that 'transsexuals are not a problem'. He stated that they have been a part and parcel of the customs and traditions of Hindu society. Citing instances from the Mahabharata, he said that LGBTQ groups existed 'ever since humans existed'. He urged that the LGBTQ people should get 'their own private space as per their wishes, and also a sense of belongingness with the rest of the society'. However, he cautioned against too much of a hullabaloo over it.

On the population question too, Bhagwat has taken the most rational stand advocating for creating awareness in society rather than resorting to laws and acts. It is well-known that demography has been a major bone of contention for Hindu groups in the country. Growing imbalance of the religious demography of the country has triggered the fear that the Hindus could become a minority in the future.

India was partitioned in 1947 on the basis of its religious demography. That has left a perpetual fear in the Hindu minds about population imbalance. Global developments like carving of East Timor from Indonesia or conflicts in Sudan and Serbia have further fortified this fear.

In India, there were reasons for this concern. The total fertility rate (TFR), the number of children a mother gives birth to, has been imbalanced among major religions in India. The official data suggests that while TFR among Hindu women is about 1.94. The TFR is 1.88 and 1.61 among Christians and Sikhs respectively, and it stands at 2.3 for Muslims. That means that the Muslim population is growing faster than the population of other religious groups. But a data point also shows that the TFR among Muslim women fell by 46 per cent in the last three decades.[5]

Bhagwat has a very logical view of this imbalance. He emphasized that not force but awareness should be the way forward to address this imbalance. 'We don't want to oppose anybody. It is not about fertility rate. More imbalance is created by religious conversions and infiltration. We noticed that the imbalance can be addressed by arresting them,' Bhagwat said in an interview.

One issue that dominated media reporting on Bhagwat's interview was about his talk of a '1000-year war'. The UNESCO constitution begins with the statement, 'wars begin in the minds of men'. Bhagwat's emphasis was actually on removing that mindset of war. It is a historical fact that India has been subjected to various political and religious aggressions over millennia. That history has left an imprint, leading to occasional aggressive outbursts in sections of the society.

Bhagwat was categorical that such aggression was uncalled for. 'It is not beneficial to be in aggression mode all the time,' he said. He even cited the example of Garibaldi to drive home that 'it is wrong to assume that those who can fight can do everything'.

Bhagwat's statement that Muslims should give up the mindset of superiority was made into a controversy by taking it out of context. He said that the attitude among some that 'we can't live with others' must be given up. He added that

[5]'National Family Health Survey (NFHS-5) 2019-21', *mohfw.gov.in*, http://tinyurl.com/bdz7dv2z. Accessed on 29 January 2024.

this mindset should be given up by everybody. 'If there is a Hindu who thinks like that, he should discard it. A communist should also shed it,' Bhagwat said.

In fact, it was the same thing that Gandhi and Nehru told Indian Muslims several times. Nehru went to Aligarh Muslim University in 1948 to ask the students whether they too feel proud of their inheritance and their ancestors, or do they 'feel alien to it and pass it by without understanding it or feeling that strange thrill'. Bhagwat asks the same questions differently.

Jesus asks Pontius Pilate to define the words before entering into an argument. Words mean differently to different people based on their prejudices and notions. Bhagwat's Bharat needs to be understood by removing the prism of such prejudices.

7

The RSS and Freedom Movement

India's independence movement had many small and big streams flowing parallel to each other. The Rashtriya Swayamsevak Sangh (RSS) too was one such stream.

Dr K.B. Hedgewar, the founder of the RSS was a prominent Congress leader in Nagpur. He was a member of the organizing committee of the annual Congress session at Nagpur in 1921, where he met Gandhi for the first time. He proposed to Gandhi that 'Purna Swaraj' or total independence should be declared as a goal. Although Gandhi did not support the idea then, the Congress had finally adopted resolution for Purna Swaraj at its Lahore session in 1929.

Despite reservations over Khilafat movement, Hedgewar joined the Civil Disobedience Movement. A fiery speaker, he was arrested in May 1921. He defended himself in the trial, listening to which, Judge Smiley complained that 'his defence was even more seditious than his original speech' and sent him to jail for nine months. When Hedgewar was released in July 1922, a public reception was organized in his honour, which was addressed by senior Congress leaders like Motilal Nehru.

The RSS was started in 1925 as a non-political, sociocultural organization. However, the volunteers were encouraged to participate in the freedom movement. The oath accorded to the RSS functionaries used to begin with the phrase '*Rashtra ko Swatantra Kar* (By Liberating the Nation)'.

During the Jungle Satyagraha in 1930, Hedgewar and 11 other colleagues were arrested and sentenced to nine months of imprisonment. The local Congress had organized a rally in support of Hedgewar. A report of the Central Provinces (CP) and Berar Police stated that Hedgewar's participation had invigorated the movement, leading to the first order against the RSS. A report of the Home Department stated, 'Of late, the Sangh has started taking interest in political movements of the country, as a result of which the CP government in their circular letter No 2352-2158 IV; dated 15/16 December 1932, was compelled to issue an order warning government servants of the communal and political nature of the Sangh, and forbidding their becoming members or participating in the organization's activities.'

The ban was challenged in the provincial legislature of CP. The government was isolated. The House leader, Raghvendra Rao, when asked about any complaints from the Muslims against the RSS, admitted that there were none. M.S. Rahman and other members praised the RSS, and the government was forced to withdraw its circular.

When the World War II broke out, the RSS refused to support the government inviting its wrath once again. In June 1939, the Home Department asked the CP government to ban the RSS using Section 16 of the Criminal Law Amendment Act. When the provincial Chief Secretary G.M. Trivedi insisted that it was not feasible, it resorted to another trick. A new ordinance under the Defence of India rules was promulgated prohibiting drills and uniforms. The obvious target was the RSS. Hundreds of RSS volunteers courted arrest against the order.

The Quit India was an important, but hastily planned movement. The RSS cadres had dominated the Congress protests during the movement in places where they were strong. In Chimur and Ashti *tehsils* of CP, the police brutality on RSS volunteers had resulted in killing some while many were sent to jail.

Many in the RSS had their sympathies with Subhas Chandra Bose's Indian National Army, increasing government's suspicion that together they might incite a revolt against the British Army. A report warned that RSS volunteers had 'infiltrated into various departments of the government such as the army, navy, post & telegraphs, railways and administrative services so that there may be no difficulty in capturing administrative departments when the time comes.' It further stated that 'the organisation is intensely anti-British, and its tone is increasingly becoming militant.'

Orders were issued for banning camps. A Home Department official, G.A. Ahmed, noted on 13 December 1943, 'This will hit the RSS most'. The training camps were raided, and cadres arrested.

As communal frenzy engulfed the country in the wake of Partition, the RSS plunged into action, saving and safely transporting the Hindus and Sikhs in Pakistan to the Indian side. Golwalkar issued directions to the volunteers that they should leave the villages only after the last of the Hindu and Sikh citizens was escorted out to safety. Many volunteers sacrificed their lives in the process.

When Gandhi came to the refugee camps in Delhi teeming with hapless millions, he was impressed by the work of the RSS volunteers. He called the RSS 'a well-organised and well-disciplined body'. In the committee formed under Maulana Azad's chairmanship to restore sanity and harmony, leaders of the RSS were also invited to join. India's freedom is the result of the efforts of many such forces. It is appropriate that all such efforts are remembered and appreciated when we celebrate the Amrit Mahotsav.

Reprinted from MALAYALA MANORAMA MAGAZINE, with permission of Malayala Manorama Co. (P) Ltd.

8

Hindutva: The Balance between Pride and Anger

On 1 January 2022, Mohan Bhagwat, sarsanghachalak of the Rashtriya Swayamsevak Sangh (RSS) addressed a gathering of eminent citizens in Bengaluru. He was there not to talk about Hindu Rashtra or about Hindu–Muslim relations, but about *paryavaran* (environment). Long considered an NGO domain, the RSS is now looking at it as an area of interest. A new wing—*paryavaran gatividhi* (climate activism)—has been added to the roster of the RSS recently.

Not just environment, the RSS-inspired NGO activism can now be found in many other areas including healthcare, education and social welfare. Saksham is one such NGO that works among the disabled, whom the RSS had christened as 'Divyang', much before the government started using that term. During the crisis of the Covid-19 pandemic, the RSS had quietly organized extensive training programmes for over a lakh of village health volunteers across the country who were given basic training by experienced doctors to tackle any future wave of the pandemic. From running primary and secondary institutions, the RSS members are now venturing into setting up universities and institutions of excellence.

Coupled with this NGO-style activism is the focussed effort to correct the image and perception. In the last 10 years or so, the RSS has quietly increased its outreach through a new activity called Vishesh Sampark—targeted outreach. All senior functionaries including Bhagwat undertake regular initiatives of reaching out to the influencers in the society to explain the cause of the RSS. The RSS chief is reaching out to leaders of the Muslim, Christian and other communities exhorting them to overcome prejudices and know the RSS from the horse's mouth.

Extending it further, the RSS has now embarked on the task of reaching out to political, academic, intellectual, religious and social leaders in dozens of countries across the world in an effort to address the disinformation challenge and affect image makeover globally.

A new confidence is conspicuous in the once reticent organization these days. This confidence stems from the fact that the core mission that it has pursued for over 10 decades—re-establishing the centrality of Hindu cultural and civilizational identity in India's national life—has now become a reality. Hindutva occupies national centre stage today. Senior Congress leader Rahul Gandhi wants to call himself a Hindu; so does the leader of the Trinamool Congress, Mamata Banerjee. Arvind Kejriwal, chief minister of Delhi, has made budget allocation for a free pilgrimage to Ayodhya for Ramlala's *darshan* (view) for all the senior citizens of the city.

It was inconceivable a decade ago. Dominant political discourse in India's post-Independence decades was centred around secularism. Hindu, Hindutva and Hinduism were relegated to the fringes and dubbed communal. Renowned Hindu Mahasabha leader N.B. Khare's description of Jawaharlal Nehru as a 'Hindu by accident' came to be identified with the mainstream polity in all these years. A false notion of secularism that got equated with the rejection of Hindu identity as majoritarianism and yet pandering to minorityism in the same breath had become the dominant political discourse after Independence.

That distorted notion of secularism, dubbed by many Hindutva protagonists as pseudo-secularism, has now been rejected by majority of Indians. To call oneself a Hindu is no longer a matter of hesitation or shame. Even prominent Congress leaders are writing books about Hindu history and civilization. No less credit for it should go to the RSS.

According to Gandhi, every movement passes through four stages: 'First they ignore you. Then they laugh at you. Then they attack you. Then you win.' Many movements lose steam during the first three stages. The RSS has successfully passed through all of them and emerged as the national mainstream, overcoming ridicule and rejection. Not many organizations have survived for a century. But the RSS has not only survived but also growing.

Besides more than 50,000 Shakhas, the RSS activity today spawns across lakhs of villages in the country. One barometer for assessing its spread and influence could be the recent campaign for mobilizing financial support for the Ram Mandir at Ayodhya. Undertaken in 2021, thousands of RSS cadres had reached out and secured support from over 13 crore Indians, that included people from all parties, social groups and even members of other religions like the Muslims and Christians. No other social organization can claim such an expansive reach and connect with the ordinary masses.

Although emerged as the fulcrum of Hindu civilizational reassertion, it is still subject to scrutiny and criticism. Its exponential growth has resulted not only in organizational spread but also in influence of its thought process, the latter many times higher than the former. In fact, the RSS outside the Shakhas is much larger than inside. And it is not necessary that the discipline found inside can be found outside too.

That puts greater onus on the RSS leadership. Mohan Bhagwat understands it. He faced sharp criticism from that section when he talked about 'common DNA of all Indians'. His original emphasis was on telling the Muslims that they were not alien to the cultural-civilizational life of this ancient nation. But when he reiterated recently that 'the DNA of all the people of India from 40,000 years ago is the same as that of the people today', it was probably his response to those angry sections, and also a likely theme for the organization in coming years.

There is widespread Hindu pride in India today, not necessarily against any other community or religion. There is also Hindu anger in some sections—a sense of persecution, genuine or otherwise—triggered by the acts like proselytism and Islamic radicalism. While pursuing its centenarian agenda, the challenge for the RSS will be to find a balance between the pride and anger, ensuring that neither spill over.

Courtesy: India Today Magazine.

9

Dharmocracy: Hindutva and Democracy

The Greeks gave the world the roots of democracy. The state as an institution was seen by ancient Greek philosophers as an instrument for moral and personal development of man. In the absence of men with morals, democracies could become a source of injustice; it was a dilemma that continued to bother the statesmen as the democratic institutions evolved over centuries in the Western world.

Deendayal Upadhyaya's view was that Western democracy was a product of this historic progression in Europe. He wrote:

> After nationalism, democracy is the second radical concept that had deeply affected European polity. In the beginning, nations were ruled by monarchs, but their tyranny led to an awakening among the people. In the wake of the Industrial Revolution and development of international commerce, the trading community became a demanding force. Naturally, the traders came into conflict with the nobility and monarchy. This conflict sowed the seeds of democracy.

Deendayal was a quintessential democrat. It is the quest for moral man that had led Deendayal to his famous philosophy of 'integral humanism'. His integral humanist philosophy was about man's evolution through society and the universe towards the divine. Deendayal's integral man was a moral man fully integrated with the cosmic reality in a progressive realization through nation and nature.

The West saw a complete separation of religion and state. 'Render unto Caesar the things that are Caesar's, and unto God, the things that are God's,' says the Bible. However, Deendayal viewed dharma not as a religion but as the eternal law that should encompass everything including statecraft. He gave a new definition to democracy based on dharma:

> Dharma is eternal. Therefore, in the definition of democracy, to say that it is a government of the people is not enough; it has to be for the good of the people. Dharma alone can decide. Therefore, a democratic government, 'Jana Rajya', must also be rooted in Dharma, i.e., a 'Dharma Rajya'. In the definition of democracy—of the people, by the people and for the people—'of' stands for independence, 'by' stands for democracy and 'for' indicates Dharma. The true democracy is one where there is freedom as well as Dharma.

Articulating the distinction between democracy of the Western origin and the dharma-based systems of India, Deendayal used to say that adult franchise and electoral process alone do not constitute democracy. He said:

> Democracy is not merely the rule of the majority. In a majoritarian government there will at least be one segment of the public whose voice has been stifled even though it may be right. This form of democracy cannot work for everyone's welfare and good. Therefore, in any form of democracy in India, election, majority and minority... all must be combined and harmonized at one pace. Anyone,

> who has a different opinion from the majority, even if he is a single individual, his viewpoint must be respected and incorporated into the governance.

This is 'Dharmocracy' or Ram Rajya.

Gandhi too expressed similar sentiments in his writings. 'The rule of majority has a narrow application, i.e., one should yield to the majority in matters of detail. But it is slavery to be amenable to the majority, no matter what its decisions are... Democracy is not a state in which people act like sheep,' he wrote in *Young India*.

After Independence, India opted for Western democratic institutions. There was scepticism in England over India's ability to govern itself. Clement Atlee, the British Prime Minister, expressed serious scepticism over India's attempts to adopt a democratic Constitution. 'The Asiatic republics are few and of recent establishment. Their record is not very encouraging. They tend to degenerate into dictatorships or oligarchies. They offer a prize for the ambitious authoritarian individual,' he warned Nehru in a letter. Yet, there was a near unanimity in India over democracy as the way forward after Independence.

In Nehru's view, democracy was the greatest gift from Europe. But leaders like B.R. Ambedkar and Deendayal viewed democracy as a natural choice for India. Speaking in the Constituent Assembly on 25 November 1949, Ambedkar reminded the members that democracies were not new to India:

> It is not that India did not know what is democracy. There was a time when India was studded with republics, and even where there were monarchies, they were either elected or limited. They were never absolute. It is not that India did not know Parliaments or Parliamentary Procedure. A study of the Buddhist Bhikshu Sanghas

> discloses that not only there were Parliaments—for, the Sanghas were nothing but Parliaments—but the Sanghas knew and observed all the rules of Parliamentary Procedure known to modern times. They had rules regarding seating arrangements, rules regarding Motions, Resolutions, Quorum, Whip, Counting of Votes, Voting by Ballot, Censure Motion, Regularization, Res Judicata, etc. Although these rules of Parliamentary Procedure were applied by the Buddha to the meetings of the Sanghas, he must have borrowed them from the rules of the Political Assemblies functioning in the country in his time.

Deendayal too would emphasize that democracy was not new to India. 'Vedic Sabhas and Samitis were also organised on the basis of democracy, and many medieval states in India were completely democratic. We have confined the powers and privileges of kings and made them cater to the demands of the public,' he wrote.

Deendayal viewed democracy as a potential tool for national unity. He also believed that for a diverse country like India, only democracy can ensure unity of the nation. 'If democracy comes to an end here, it will spell the doom of national unity,' he averred, adding, 'even secessionist and separatist forces will gradually move towards national unity in a democracy. Even when they win the elections on the basis of casteism and regionalism, they would realise that they cannot sit alone in the legislatures. Democracy is essential for national unity.'

Both Gandhi and Deendayal opined that the success of democracy lay in educating the masses and failure to do so will lead to democracy degenerating into a mobocracy. Deendayal used to refer to William Shakespeare's *Julius Caesar* to underscore the nature of the unenlightened public opinion.

When Brutus murdered Julius Caesar the Roman public had celebrated it, but when Antony revealed Brutus' deception, they went after Brutus the next moment. 'It is difficult to keep democracy alive between the two forms of government—mobocracy and autocracy,' Deendayal averred.

Plato too had entertained similar fears about democracy. Demagogues can indulge in 'false and braggart words' and turn democracies into staging points for tyranny, he feared. That democracies can end up producing tyrants and authoritarian dictators was the experience of the world in the last few centuries.

Authoritarians abhor rational debate and reason. They revel in their own superciliousness and narcissism. Julius Caesar used to invite sculptors to prepare hundreds of his own sculptures.

Whenever he came across a new name, Stalin's only question used to be as to whether that new individual was a 'genius'. If the answer was 'yes', that individual would disappear the next day.

In her book *Twilight of Democracy*, American author and journalist Anne Applebaum refers to Hannah Arendt as 'the original philosopher of totalitarianism', who identified the authoritarian personality as a 'radically lonely individual who, without any social ties to family, friends, comrades or mere acquaintances, derives his sense of having a place in the world only from his belonging to a movement, his membership in the party'.

That was why 'that people should be trained as good citizens for democracies to succeed' has been an accepted proposition all over the world. The responsibility for it was put on the leadership—the philosopher kings. Ronald Reagan, the fortieth president of the United States, used to say that a good leader is one who makes his people do good things. 'The greatest leader is not necessarily the one who does the greatest things. He is the one who gets the people to do the greatest things,' he said.

Deendayal viewed it from a different perspective. While acknowledging the need for creating 'popular moral authority', he would still argue that it cannot be done by the rulers alone. Left to them, the rulers would like to brainwash the public into believing only in them. 'In India, the problem has been solved by taking away the right of building democracy from the government. Educating public opinion is the work of selfless ascetics. Ruling according to public opinion is the task of the government. The ascetics always have the upliftment of the public and their spiritual interests in mind, and, as such, they work according to these noble ideals,' Deendayal explained. He called those noble ideals *sanskaras*. People should be imbued with ideals like feeling for the nation, consciousness of their responsibility and discipline, he said, warning that if these sanskaras were absent in the citizens, democracy would 'degenerate into an instrument of individual, class and party interest'.

Deendayal noticed growing evils like money power and muscle power in Indian politics in the initial years after independence itself and cautioned that it would sound a death knell for democracy. He insisted that parties should put up candidates who were selfless and committed to public service. They should discourage the use of money power to influence the voters. Deendayal bluntly said that 'there is not a single political party in India that is worried about this. The only thing that matters to them is that their candidate must somehow win... They only grant a ticket to the candidate who has the maximum chances of winning'.

He then turned his attention to the people and called upon them to remember that 'an ineligible candidate is not worthy of our vote even if he belongs to a good political party. It is possible that while granting the ticket to such a person, a political party may have been guided by immediate gains or it may even have made a grave mistake. It is, therefore, the duty of a responsible voter to rectify this mistake by his awareness'. As a leader of Jana Sangh, Deendayal never allowed such things.

Like Ambedkar, Deendayal too feared that democracies, in the absence of such public awareness, could breed dictatorial tendencies in the leaders. He was a staunch votary of democratic decentralization. 'The centralization of political, economic and social powers in one individual or institution is a hindrance in the way of democracy,' he believed.

Deendayal's idealism is a tall order for present-day politics. But it is key to the survival of democracy. As Noam Chomsky pointed out, democracy is not merely an ideal to be valued, it is essential for our survival.

Reprinted from OPEN MAGAZINE, with permission of Open Media Network Pvt. Ltd.

10

The Sangh and Modernity

The Rashtriya Swayamsevak Sangh (RSS) is an idea that is still evolving. Founded in 1925 and nearing its centenary, it is still growing. Very few non-governmental organizations survive for such a long time. It remains an enigma to many. It has its detractors, mainly among the liberal intelligentsia and the left academia. There are people among India's minority community who harbour apprehensions about its intentions, and it has vast cross-sections of Indian society that admire and adore it. At the end of the day, it can be abhorred or admired, but it cannot be ignored.

Not Ideology, but an Evolving Idea

'All ideologies are idiotic, whether religious or political, for, it is conceptual thinking, the conceptual world, which has so unfortunately divided man,' bemoaned Indian philosopher Jiddu Krishnamurti. Europe was the mother of ideologies—from Adam Smith's capitalism to the social conservatism of Thomas Hobbes and John Locke to the liberalism of John Stuart Mill to the communism of Karl Marx. These ideologies have resulted in schisms in the world, as Krishnamurti pointed out. The American historian and social thinker Morris Berman had warned that 'an idea is something you have; an ideology is something that has you'.

India has historically been the land of ideas. From the Vedic times through Mahavira, Buddha, Shankara, Aurobindo, Vivekananda and Gandhi, the great men of India have only been philosophers, articulating profound ideas for the welfare of mankind.

The RSS, too, was born not with an ideology but as an idea. When Keshav Baliram Hedgewar, the medical doctor from Nagpur and a Congressite freedom fighter, founded the organization on Vijayadashami in 1925, it did not have a name or a constitution. The name came through deliberations among the original members after a couple of months. The constitution came only after a couple of decades, in 1949.

The RSS, in essence, is a constantly evolving idea. It has a twin vision—individual perfection at the micro level and social cohesion and unity at the macro level. It changed with the times, adopted new things and adapted to new situations, but it never let go of the focus from its twin vision. Critics mistook the RSS to be a fossilized body of obscurantists stuck in a time warp. But, as pointed out by author Badri Narayan in his recent book *Republic of Hindutva: How the Sangh Is Reshaping Indian Democracy*, it is the critics that are stuck in that time warp in their understanding of the organization.

The Twin Vision of Hindutva

The initial idea that inspired Hedgewar and his young band of followers was a simple one. India suffered slavery not because of lack of strength but because of lack of individual character and social unity. Even B.R. Ambedkar had talked about it in his famous 'Three Warnings' speech in the Constituent Assembly. 'It is not that India was never an independent country. The point is that she once lost the independence she had. Will she lose it a second time? What perturbs me greatly is the fact that not only India has once before lost her independence, but she lost it by the infidelity and treachery of some of her own people,' Ambedkar had said.

Hedgewar too had held a similar understanding of Indian history. At the time of its inception, he gave two goals to the organization: one, to organize Hindu society at the local level; and two, to strive for independence. Those were the times when many national leaders believed that Hindu social reform was an essential part of the nationalist movement. Bal Gangadhar Tilak strove for it; Madan Mohan Malaviya worked for it; Veer Savarkar and Ambedkar agitated for it; and Gandhi made it an integral part of the Independence struggle.

The simple twin vision of Hedgewar was given greater philosophical finesse by his successor M.S. Golwalkar, also known as Guruji. Hedgewar was a revolutionary and freedom fighter, and hence his thrust was sociopolitical. Golwalkar was an ascetic, trained in the Ramakrishna Mission. He gave a dharmic, semi-spiritual orientation to the organization. Through his 33-year leadership, Golwalkar gave a philosophical locus for the idea of the RSS.

The culmination of the independence movement was the liberation of India, but the leadership's failure in preserving national, emotional and territorial integrity had led the evolution of the idea of the RSS to a second stage. Golwalkar decided to give pre-eminence to the mission of alleviating Ambedkar's apprehensions about India losing its independence a second time and averting future partitions. He got the idea of the RSS transfused with the age-old cultural and civilizational identity of India, which he described as the Hindu Rashtra. Such an overarching identity can only sustain the emotional and territorial integrity of the nation, he averred. Articulations like Radha Kumud Mukherjee's book *The Fundamental Unity of India* (1914) to Bankim Chandra Chattopadhyay's poem

'Vande Mataram' (included in his 1882 novel *Anandamath*) to Gandhi's Ram Rajya had all expressed the same spirit.

Inclusive, Not Exclusive

There was hardly any dispute over India's cultural oneness until the Muslim League came up with the dubious construct that the 'Hindu identity meant anti-Muslim'. The defensive few among the Congress leadership had accepted this false narrative in their anxiety to appease Muhammad Ali Jinnah and the Muslim League. The leftist intelligentsia had further fuelled this misnomer. But proponents like Golwalkar and Savarkar had never agreed with that hypothesis and insisted upon the inclusive character of the concept of Hindu identity.

In his 1923 work titled *Essentials of Hindutva*, Savarkar talked about the suspicion that 'crept into the minds of some of our well-meaning but hasty countrymen that the origin of the words Hindu and Hindusthan is to be traced to the malice of the Mohammedans' and called it 'singularly stupid'. 'Long before Mohammad was born, nay, long before the Arabians were heard of as a people, this ancient nation was known to ourselves as well as to the foreign world by the proud epithet Sindhu or Hindu,' he wrote.

Golwalkar too was categorical in dismissing the propaganda that the RSS was out to convert all to Hinduism. In an interview to a visiting Iranian scholar, Saifuddin Jeelany, in 1971, Golwalkar said:

> Let us all realise that we are all the children of this soil, and we must have our allegiance to this land. We belong to the same society and that our ancestors are common. That our aspirations are also common. Understanding this is Indianisation in the real sense. Indianisation does

> not mean that one should be asked to quit his religious system. We neither said this, nor we are going to say so.

Going further, Golwalkar insisted, 'Follow your own religion. The God of Islam, Christianity and Hinduism is the same and we are all His devotees. Give people true knowledge of Islam. Give people true knowledge of Hinduism. Educate them to know that all religions teach men to be selfless, holy and pious. Indianisation does not mean making all people Hindus.'

Golwalkar was not alone in insisting on the 'common ancestry' and 'common aspirations' for all Indians. In a passionate speech to the students of the Aligarh Muslim University in 1948, Prime Minister Jawaharlal Nehru had exhorted:

> I have said that I am proud of our inheritance and our ancestors who gave an intellectual and cultural pre-eminence to India. How do you feel about the past? Do you feel that you are also the sharers in it and inheritors of it, and therefore proud of something that belongs to you as much as to me? Or do you feel alien to it and pass it by without understanding it or feeling that strange thrill which comes from the realisation that we are the trustees and inheritors of this vast treasure? You are Muslim and I am a Hindu. We may adhere to different religious faiths or even none; but that does not take us away from that cultural inheritance that is yours as well as mine. The past holds us together; why should the present or the future divide us in spirit?

The reported assertion of the RSS chief Mohan Bhagwat in 2018—'If we do not accept Muslims, it's not Hindutva. Hindutva is Indianness and inclusion'—should put to rest various criticisms of the core philosophy of Hindutva.

A Bottom-up Leadership Model

From Gandhi and Ambedkar to Pranab Mukherjee, many who had a first-hand experience of the RSS were baffled by its organizational ability and disciplined rise. The RSS is undoubtedly the world's largest non-governmental body today, with over 60,000 daily meeting Shakhas (branches)[6] and dozens of allied organizations described as the Sangh Parivar. Its cadre run more than two lakh service activities and about 25,000 schools. Its members occupy high positions in politics and public life.

Yet, this gigantic organization runs in a nondescript and smooth manner. It has not split even once, nor there was any leadership tussle ever. Successive sarsanghchalaks—the chiefs of the organization—appointed their successors, not necessarily the seniormost leaders, without any fuss. When Golwalkar, a relatively new entrant and just 35 years of age, was picked by Hedgewar to succeed him in 1940, several members went to Hedgewar's senior-most follower Appaji Joshi insisting that he should become the chief. Appaji Joshi's reply was typical of the organizational culture that RSS had nurtured. He was, no doubt, the right-hand man of Hedgewar, Joshi told the members, adding that 'Golwalkar was Hedgewar's heart'. I vividly remember an incident when K.S. Sudarshan succeeded as the sarsanghchalak in March 2000 at Nagpur. Atal Bihari Vajpayee was the prime minister and hence the succession in RSS was keenly watched by the media. They accosted H.V. Seshadri, who was senior to Sudarshan and regarded by many as the natural successor of Rajendra Singh, asking him whether he was disappointed. Seshadri looked at them and said in all

[6]'RSS Top Brass Discusses Ways to Start 35K New Shakhas in Next One-And-A-Half Years', *Hindustan Times*, 17 October 2022, http://tinyurl.com/5x4j3rbb. Accessed on 27 December 2023.

humility, 'I am not qualified to be the chief.'

That the most powerful position of the head of the RSS can change hands so naturally is unimaginable in the present political milieu. The RSS leadership is revered. Yet, the real power lies in its unique organizational structure. Like the Jain philosophy of Anekantavada, the RSS structure is a complex web and true power lies with multiple grassroots unit. Like Sun Tzu's philosophy of 'the art of war', it keeps multiple targets to achieve its objective. Like the republics of the medieval era, it built a strong culture of collective leadership at the top and abhorred individual supremacy. Apart from the first two chiefs, the RSS has resisted the temptation of according any special status to other leaders.

It built a fascinating bottom-up leadership model. Its cadre at the grassroots wear PPE kits as effortlessly as they wear their uniforms. They reach out to tribes living in remote jungles as enthusiastically as they approach software professionals in a metropolitan city.

Decentralism and collective decision-making form the core of the RSS's organizational functioning. Some find it frustrating and insist that the RSS was too slow to respond to situations. One senior political leader had once compared the RSS to a tortoise. A turtle is never in a hurry. It keeps its pace. When attacked, it simply withdraws its limbs under its shell. This analogy is inaccurate. The RSS has always been one of the first responders in times of crises. In achieving its targets too, the organization has a commendable record.

Karl Marx and Friedrich Engels had authored *The Communist Manifesto* in 1848, but it took 70 years for the first communist government to be established by Lenin in Russia. Liberal ideas took much longer to find coherent manifestation. Comparatively, the turtle in India has done well. Its members were in government by 1977 and were leading in many areas of public life by the stroke of the new century.

The turtle analogy can perhaps be applied to its response to criticism in the past. The RSS was subjected to unjust criticism for decades and stereotyped as fascist, Hitlerian, and so on. For many decades, the RSS did not choose to respond in any conventional way. 'To know the RSS, be in the RSS' was its response. Over the last three decades, however, the organization has built a robust mechanism for public engagement and propaganda.

A fascinating journey of over nine decades has brought the RSS out of the fringes of Indian society onto the national centre stage today. A journalist once confessed to me some years ago that as a liberal, he considered the RSS as the greatest enemy of India: 'I used to think that you are a lunatic fringe, and it is my duty to expose you. After criticising you as a fringe element for two decades, here I am, interviewing you on my channel. You have become the mainstream and we the fringe.'

Sociocultural vs Sociopolitical

The real challenge that the RSS faced was not ideological or organizational but political. The first major political attack came in the form of allegations of involvement in Gandhi's murder. The *pind*—core ethos—of the RSS, when Hedgewar established it, was sociopolitical. It was Golwalkar who sought to transform it into a sociocultural one after Independence. A debate ensued wherein some seniors like Balasaheb Deoras, who was to succeed Golwalkar in 1973, and his brother Bhaurao, disagreed with Golwalkar's insistence on staying away from active politics and even left the organization for a couple of years. But in his long 33-year stewardship, Golwalkar had firmly established that principle although some senior members were loaned to Syama Prasad Mukherjee's Bharatiya Jana Sangh.

Golwalkarite sociocultural identity, to which the RSS is wedded to this day, has helped the organization reap enormous goodwill. Despite initial ideological differences, Nehru found the RSS to be virtuous enough to march shoulder-to-shoulder with the Indian Army at the Republic Day parade in 1963. Over 2,500 RSS volunteers had participated in the march upon the invitation of the government. Lal Bahadur Shastri had invited Golwalkar to discuss about support during the Indo-Pakistan War of 1965. Golwalkar's demise was condoled in Parliament. Indira Gandhi paid her tribute, saying, 'Shri Golwalkar, an eminent personality who was not a member of the House, is no more. He held a respected position in national life by his force of personality and the intensity of his conviction, even though many of us could not agree with him.'

Two important events in the last quarter of the last century impacted the RSS's identity profoundly. First was Emergency (1975–77). Banned by the government, the Sangh had launched a massive Satyagraha against Indira Gandhi. Thousands of RSS cadres had been asked to fight for a cause primarily linked to their constitutional rights. In 1948, they had held a Satyagraha against the Government for erasing the blemish of Gandhi's murder. But Satyagraha during Emergency was a different affair. The sociocultural had to don the mantle of the sociopolitical. The formation of the Janata Party in 1977 and its collapse on the RSS question in 1980 had drawn the RSS further into the political vortex.

The 1980s saw the rise of the Ram Janmabhoomi movement with serious historical and political overtones. The RSS took a conscious decision to plunge into it in the mid-1980s after assessing its implications for the organization. Incidentally, it was Balasaheb Deoras who was at the helm during both these transformative events. The fight against Indira Gandhi's dictatorship and a decade-long agitation for

Ram Janmabhoomi had established the new credentials of the RSS as a mainstream social organization—as not only a cultural but an influential political voice. The RSS had challenged pseudo-Western notions like faulty secularism and succeeded in transforming the Indian political landscape from Nehruvian nationalism to cultural nationalism.

Like America, India too is a 'Right Nation'. '*Dharma Praana Bharata* (Dharma is the soul of India)' was proclaimed by Swami Vivekananda more than a century ago. Gandhi and the RSS firmly believed in this basic national character of India. The post-Independence efforts to superimpose a West-inspired superstructure on an essentially religious soil did not succeed much. The shaky superstructure gradually came down by the end of the last century and the essential cultural core of India has started manifesting in all walks of public life. The stigma once attached to the word 'Hindu' is no longer there today nor is the castigation of 'Hindu' as communal. Instead, the discourse is about who are real Hindus: the RSS or its detractors? No little credit can go to the RSS for this fundamental transformation.

In the process, the RSS has shed its reticent and enigmatic demeanour and come out more openly in the sociopolitical arena. From economic policies to border challenges, from environmental issues to homosexuality debates, nothing is anathema anymore. With its vast organizational network, greater engagement with the world outside and adaptation to new technologies, the RSS has emerged as a pre-eminent voice that echoes across the country.

The immediate and major beneficiary of the transformed sociopolitical landscape was the Bharatiya Janata Party (BJP) with which the RSS shares an umbilical cord and also human resources. Once considered only a part of the wider Sangh Parivar, the BJP has grown into a behemoth. The two organizations maintain a respectable distance at the top, on the principle of 'consultative non-interference'. While sharing human resources with the Jana Sangh, Golwalkar had envisioned a relationship like that of the two rails of a railway track which never meet but never go apart either. The prospect of the sociopolitical overpowering the sociocultural down the organizational hierarchy is not imaginary anymore and the RSS leadership is conscious of that critical challenge. Upholding the moral authority of the latter and ensuring that the political arm steadies itself in the storm of realpolitik is a task that requires humungous skill and acumen on the part of the Sangh leadership.

The Challenge of the Future

The Golwalkarite sociocultural agenda having been largely achieved and established in India's mainstream, the RSS has to now move to the next level that involves systemic reform. Deendayal Upadhyaya talked about it in his treatise on 'integral humanism'. India's mindset could be purged of non-coherent Western concepts and ideas but the institutions and inheritance that the colonialists left behind are still intact. The centrifugal forces that those institutions release—caste conflicts, communal politics, regional and linguistic chauvinism, alien governance models and inept administrative structures—continue to pose a challenge. They appear dormant today because the idea of the RSS has been suffused with state power to give it a greater power and aura. As the state power diminishes, these forces will rear their ugly heads once again.

Within the broader contours of India's Constitution, the RSS has to strive to infuse various sectors like education, governance, jurisprudence and social systems with nobler Indian ideas. Such an endeavour requires enormous public support and participation. The youth of India, the majority of its population, are proud nationals at one level and globalized citizens at another. Modernity and prosperity are the mantra for them.

The RSS is the only force that has the potential to become the epicentre of their hopes and aspirations, provided it diligently rebuilds its image and agenda.

Reprinted from OPEN MAGAZINE, with permission of Open Media Network Pvt. Ltd.

11

A Model for Managing Hindu Temples

Kashi is an ancient city, 'older than history, older than tradition, older even than legend' as American writer Mark Twain described it. Sage Vyasa had compiled the Vedas sitting on the banks of River Ganga in this holy city. The Pandava brothers had visited this city founded by Lord Shiva. Skanda Purana gives an elaborate description of this holy city. From Buddha to Shankara to Guru Nanak—every spiritual leader had his footprints etched on Kashi's sacred soil.

The Kashi Vishwanath Temple is utmost sacred; it is home to a 'Jyotirlinga' or Lord Shiva in the form of a radiant light—considered by millions as a 'crossing place' or a *'tirtha'*—'between this world and the "far shore" of the transcendent Brahman,' as eminent American scholar Diana Eck puts it.

The temple had repeatedly witnessed destruction during the iconoclastic invasions of Muhammad Ghori, Sikandar Lodhi and finally Aurangzeb. Aurangzeb's destruction also saw a mosque rising over the ruins of the ancient temple.

Like a sphinx, the temple had bounced back to life after every demolition. Raja Man Singh and Raja Todar Mal, the two generals in Akbar's court, were credited for rebuilding the temple towards the end of the fifteenth century. After Aurangzeb's destruction, Maharaja Malhar Rao Holkar, the ruler of Indore and Maharaja of Jaipur had attempted to restore it unsuccessfully in the middle of the eighteenth century. Finally, Malhar Rao's daughter-in-law and the famed ruler of Indore, Rani Ahilya Bai Holkar, succeeded in rebuilding the temple next to the mosque in 1780. Since then, this magnificent temple has been serving the seekers uninterruptedly.

'*Ibadat khana e naqoosian ast—hama na kaaba e Hindustan ast* (This is a place of worship where people make music from conch shells; this truly is the Kaaba of Hindustan),' Mirza Ghalib writes in his poem 'Chirag-e-Dair' or 'The Lamp in the Temple'. Another poet, Allama Iqbal, had found in Ganga the pride of our civilizational caravan. '*Ai aab rooy e Ganga, woh din hain yaad tujhko, utra tere kinare jub karavaan hamara?* (O Ganga, our very pride is bound with you; Do you remember our caravan, which rested on your banks forever?),' he wrote. Also, who can forget the soothing tunes of Ustad Bismillah Khan's mesmerising shehnai in the temple precincts!

Like the deniers of Holocaust in the West, there are iconoclasm-deniers in India too. Historian K.N. Panikkar had come up with the whitewashed narrative that Aurangzeb's destruction of the Kashi Vishwanath Temple had 'political motives', while B.N. Pande peddled the bizarre theory that Aurangzeb had done it out of rage because the temple priests had kidnapped and dishonoured a Hindu princess of his entourage in the basement 'beneath Lord Jagannath's seat'. The proof of this was placed in certain manuscripts in the possession of an unknown mullah of Lucknow. Neither the manuscript nor the mullah ever surfaced. In fact, history shows that Aurangzeb had never travelled to the East and never visited Kashi. Moreover, the entry in Maasir-i-Alamgiri, the court chronicle of Aurangzeb on 2 September 1669 categorically states: 'News came to court that in accordance with the emperor's command his officers had demolished the temple of Vishwanath in Benaras'.

In response to these negationist narratives of the 'eminent historians', some insist that the historical wrongs must be avenged in the same way. In 1740s, Raja Malhar Rao had attempted to remove the mosque and build the temple exactly on that location. But the intervention of Nawab of Awadh had prevented it. Should that eighteenth-century path be applied in the twenty-first century? In the case of Ayodhya, none had supported the demolition in 1992, although it paved the way for a resolution three decades later. Babri was a non-functioning mosque structure under which a functioning temple had existed. Also, the Places of Worship Act came into existence, which prohibited the raising of any other such disputes.

Gandhi was in Kashi in February 1916 for the foundation laying ceremony of the Benaras Hindu University. Anguished at what he witnessed during a visit to the Kashi Vishwanath Temple, he poured his heart out saying: 'Is not this great temple a reflection of our own character? I speak feelingly, as a Hindu. Is it right that the lanes of our sacred temple should be as dirty as they are? If even our temples are not models of roominess and cleanliness, what can our self-government be?'

Rani Ahilya Bai Holkar had not been able to replace the mosque but built a glorious temple in the vicinity. What we had done to that temple in just a century calls for urgent introspection. It needed the resolve of Prime Minister Modi to bring back its order and glory after 240 years. Gandhi had suggested that the temples must be transformed into 'abodes of holiness, cleanliness and peace' immediately after Independence. What happened to many temples was just the opposite.

Courtesy: India Today Digital.

12

Ram: A Universal Deity

Ram's greatest qualities that made him *Maryada Purushottam* were manifested not when he was in Ayodhya, the centre of power, but when in exile in the forests.

It is said that there would not be a village in India without a Ram temple. As historian William Dalrymple puts it, Ram is a universal deity, 'treasured as the common property of every Hindu – as well as that of many Muslims, Sikhs, Buddhists, Jains, and Christians'. It is easy to relate to Ram, because, as aptly described by sage Valmiki, he was an avatar of Vishnu as well as an ordinary, yet ideal human being. It is this relatability that has made Ram and the Ramayana the most popular epic hero and epic poem in the world respectively. Robert Goldman, a Sanskrit professor from University of California observes, 'Few works of literature produced in any place at any time have been as popular, influential, imitated and successful as the great and ancient Sanskrit epic poem, the Valmiki Ramayana.'

All religions, Semitic or Eastern, have sacredness attached to spaces and heroes. The Romanian scholar of religion at the University of Chicago, Mircea Eliade, had coined the term 'hierophany', meaning the sacredness attached to places brushed by God's presence. For the Jews, the Wailing Wall in Jerusalem, believed to belong to the temple built by King

Solomon in tenth century is sacred, while it is Jerusalem for the Christians, because of its association with Jesus from childhood until after the resurrection. For the Muslims, Mecca is sacred as the birthplace of the prophet. Even the Greeks still attach sacredness to classical Greek sites like the shrine of Apollo at Delphi or the temple of Artemis at Ephesus, the ancient Greek city, now in Turkey.

In the same manner, Hindu deities too have their sacred history and places. Hindu gods are the primary unifiers of the Hindu nation. Ram and Krishna, the greatest epic heroes of Hinduism, traversed the length and breadth of Bharat. Ram journeyed from north to south, while Krishna travelled from west to east (and also from Mathura to Dwaraka in Gujarat). Numerous sacred places dot the geography of India linked to the history of these two hallowed figures. Temples were built for them, and in some cases, by them too. The deity of Shiva in Rameswaram in South India is believed to have been installed by Shri Ram himself.

These temples represent their connection with gods at one level, while they diffuse noble values that the gods represented. It is that hoary value system that binds the Hindu society together. Ram Manohar Lohia, the eminent socialist thinker of the last century, regarded Ram, Krishna and Shiva as the greatest symbols of the ancient Indic civilization. 'You stand outside any temple dedicated to them. You will find a mini Hindustan there,' he used to say. From Kashi, Mathura and Ayodhya in the north to Tirupati and Rameswaram in the south, from Guwahati in the far east to Dwaraka in the far west, every place dedicated to them is sacred to Indians.

Lohia's Ram was an ideal human being. Swami Vivekananda too described Ram as 'the embodiment of truth, of morality, the ideal son, the ideal husband, and above all, the ideal king'. For Mahatma Gandhi, Ram enshrined truthfulness.

In the 'Aranya Kanda' (the forest episode) of the Ramayana, the demon Mareecha, when asked by Ravana to disguise as a golden deer to distract Ram, warns Ravana against the misadventure by describing Ram as रामो विग्रहवान धर्मस्साधुस्सत्यपराक्रम:—meaning, Ram was the embodiment of dharma; a pious man with truth as his power.

Valmiki used two phrases to describe the ideal human being, Ram—'Vigrahvaan Dharmah' and 'Maryadaa Purushottam'—epitome of dharma and morals.

Ram became great not when he was ruling, but when he was struggling. Virtuous are those who are undisturbed when out of power. Ram's greatest qualities that made him Maryada Purushottam were manifested not when he was in Ayodhya, the seat of royal power, but when in exile in the forests. His finest qualities of humility, magnanimity and fortitude came out during various incidents of the *vanvas* (life in the forest). Ram's high point was his respect for Ravan. He bows before him in reverence for his scholarship when they come face to face on the battlefield on the first day. When Ravan is on his deathbed, Ram sends Lakshman to learn some noble lessons. Lakshman comes back saying that Ravan refused to teach any. Having learned the minute details of the meeting, Ram scolds Lakshman for standing at Ravan's head and sends him back with the instruction that he should beseech guidance by standing at Ravan's feet.

Ram's low point was when he asked Sita to undergo *Agni Pariksha* (fire test). According to Ram, society needs to be convinced about her chastity. Sita admonishes him for a lack of manliness. But for Ram, 'people first' was Ram Rajya, as Gandhi described it.

Hinduism is a worship-centric religion. Everything, animate and inanimate alike, is worshipped here. Sacredness of everything in creation, the omnipresence of divinity, is the essence of Hinduism. Power, for Ram, was also an object of worship. Sage Valmiki used two significant phrases in Ramayana to describe Ram's rule. They were—'Raamo Raajyamupaasitva' (Ram worshipped his kingdom) and 'Aaraadhanaaya Lokasya' (worship of the people). When time came to leave Sita forever, Ram says:

स्नेहं दयां च सौख्यं च यदि वा जानकीमपि।
आराधनाय लीकस्य मुँचतो नास्ति में व्यथा।।

(For the worship of my people, I can leave my love, kindness, all kinds of pleasures and even Sita)

Ram was known for his affection and kindness. Ram and Sita are held as the epitome of love. Yet, Ram says that he was ready to give up his most important qualities, not for the sake of power, but '*Aaradhanaya Lokasya*'—to worship people.

There are many great lessons that one can learn from Ram and Ramayana. But the greatest is reserved for the rulers—humility, not arrogance of power, is the way to worship the kingdom and people. That was the kind of Ram Rajya that Gandhi wanted for India post-Independence. He wrote in *Harijan* in January 1937:

> By political independence I do not mean an imitation to the British House of commons, or the soviet rule of Russia or the Fascist rule of Italy or the Nazi rule of Germany. They have systems suited to their genius. We must have ours suited to ours. What that can be is more than I can tell. I have described it as Ramarajya i.e., sovereignty of the people based on pure moral authority.

Reprinted from CHINTAN–INDIA FOUNDATION BLOGS, with permission of India Foundation.

13

The Integral Man

Making a 'moral man' has been the quest of the philosophers for centuries. Some believed that God and religion can help achieve that; some believed in man's ability for reason. In the Old Testament of Ecclesiastes, King Solomon finds man's moral virtue to be just to 'fear God and keep his commandments'. But later, the Enlightenment thinkers insisted upon man's innate wisdom and his power of understanding as the basis of his virtue.

The Greeks gave the world the roots of democracy. But the early Greek philosophers too struggled with the question of individual morality and social happiness. In *The Federalist Papers*, James Madison, one of the founding fathers of the American Constitution and the fourth President of the United States, highlights this serious democratic dilemma:

> If men were angels, no government would be necessary. If angels were to govern men, neither external nor internal controls on government would be necessary. In framing a government which is to be administered by men over men, the greatest difficulty lies in this: you must first enable the government to control the governed; and in the next place oblige it to control itself.

Plato's answer to this dilemma was to have 'philosopher kings'. Plato argued that either the philosophers should become kings, or the rulers should 'genuinely and adequately philosophize' for greater public happiness. Enlightenment thinkers like Kant believed in the power of human understanding. *Sapere aude*, the Latin phrase meaning 'dare to be wise' became the motto of Enlightenment thinking. Reason was the God for the Enlightenment thinkers.

This quest for the moral man had led to many experiments in the Western world. The philosopher king idea, while allowing for some wise men to rule over their subjects judiciously in the name of God, also created dictators like Hitler and Mussolini. But when reason became God, the Bastille was invaded by French citizens in July 1789 to set off the famous French Revolution. God was stripped of 'His Holiness' and reason occupied his place. 'One god only, Le Peuple (The People),' the French revolutionaries declared, paving the way for the subsequent rise of both the Communist ideology and the democratic institutions. The Western civilization finally settled for a religious and moral narrative, which Martin Luther King Jr had beautifully summed up by saying 'The arc of the moral universe is long, but it bends towards justice'.

It is this same quest that led Deendayal Upadhyaya, a forgotten scholar and politician of the last century and one of the founding fathers of the Bharatiya Jana Sangh and later its president, to his famous philosophy of 'integral humanism'. Deendayal grew up in the moralist tradition of the Rashtriya Swayamsevak Sangh (RSS), and hence for him, everything in life was based on moral principles of yore. Unlike the Western philosophical thinkers, Deendayal did not find religion and reason to be opposite poles. His integral humanist philosophy was about man's evolution through society and the universe towards the divine. He did not see man, society, nature and the ultimate reality in compartments or as concentric circles. It was an evolutionary spiral according to him, defining man's journey.

Interestingly, the concept of the spiral by which the universe was described as the one without any beginning or end is not just an ancient Hindu thought. Many other ancient cultures too believed in the beginning-less and end-less history. The Greeks saw the universe to be continuously moving in a circular fashion—growing, decaying and recurring. For the Babylonians, 'past, present and future were all part of one continuous stream of events in heaven and earth. Gods and men continued ad infinitum'. The Native Americans had a circular, 'cyclical, no-beginning, no-end, turn-and-turn-again, mythic view of reality'. Even in Buddhism, time is without beginning and without end.

Deendayal's integral man was a moral man fully integrated with the cosmic reality in a progressive realization through nation and nature. Four-fold arrangements are unique to Hindu culture. Deendayal based his entire philosophy on these four-fold arrangements. At the individual level, he averred that the integral progress of man is possible through the 'four-fold responsibilities of catering to the needs of body, mind, intellect and soul'. At the level of society, the essence of Deendayal's integral way was to satisfy the human longings for 'Dharma, Artha, Kama and Moksha'.

The West has seen man, society and nature in compartments and found inherent conflict in their intersectional interaction. Deendayal's integral humanism proposes a fundamental unity in the entire creation. That fundamental unity can be experienced through dharma. Deendayal dwelt at length on the uniquely Indian concept of dharma and described it as the 'innate law'.

The West saw a complete separation of religion and state—'Render unto Caesar the things that are Caesar's, and unto God, the things that are God's,' said the Bible. However, Deendayal viewed dharma not as a religion but as the eternal law that should encompass everything including the statecraft. Deendayal argued:

> Dharma is eternal. Therefore, in the definition of democracy, to say that it is a government of the people is not enough; it has to be for the good of the people. Dharma alone can decide. Therefore, a democratic government, 'Jana Rajya', must also be rooted in Dharma, i.e. a 'Dharma Rajya'. In the definition of democracy—of the people, by the people and for the people—'of' stands for independence, 'by' stands for democracy and 'for' indicates Dharma. The true democracy is one where there is freedom as well as Dharma.

In essence, while the West's quest was for a moral man and the debates and disputes that ensued were over whether religion can create one or reason, Deendayal's mantra was for an integral human—an evolutionary integration of man with nation and nature on the principles of dharma, the eternal moral virtues.

Reprinted from CHINTAN–INDIA FOUNDATION BLOGS, with permission of India Foundation.

LEARNINGS FROM HISTORY

'Instead of making history, we are made by history'[7]

—MARTIN LUTHER KING JR

---

7 '"Transformed Nonconformist"', *Stanford: The Martin Luther King, Jr. Research and Education Institute*, http://tinyurl.com/fc4ymevy. Accessed on 8 January 2024.

14

History Lessons for Rahul Gandhi

On 6 December 1273, a famous Catholic saint, Thomas Aquinas, went into a final trance. Aquinas is remembered for his medieval endeavour to inject rationalism into Catholic theology. Reason and reform were the core of Thomistic thought. After facing a lot of criticism, Aquinas was finally canonized as a saint by the Vatican after 50 years. 6 December is also the *Mahaparinirvan* day (death anniversary) of the Indian reformist leader B.R. Ambedkar. Like Aquinas, Ambedkar too fought for reason in religion. He too faced rejection but finally found his place in history.

Ambedkar continues to be at the centre of a legacy battle. During his Bharat Jodo Yatra at Mhow in Madhya Pradesh, the birthplace of Ambedkar, Congress leader Rahul Gandhi accused the Rashtriya Swayamsevak Sangh (RSS) of showing false sympathy for him and 'backstabbing' him.

These allegations smack of an urge to appropriate the legacy of a great reformer and deny it to others. Before talking about backstabbing, it may be important to ponder over the 'front stab' that Ambedkar had to endure at the hands of the Congress leadership not just while he was alive but even after his death.

When Ambedkar breathed his last on 6 December 1956, Prime Minister Jawaharlal Nehru rose in the Rajya Sabha to deliver an obituary address. Paying glowing tributes to the deceased is a custom in obituary addresses. But Nehru's address was different. 'Ambedkar, from many years, had been a very controversial figure,' Nehru contended, insinuating that he pursued convictions 'with rather greater intensity than perhaps required.' While Ambedkar was the 'symbol' of the intense feeling of the suppressed classes in India, 'some of us thought' that he 'overdid the expression of that feeling', Nehru said in an accusatory tone.[8]

Leaders of the Congress should know this aversion of their leadership to accepting and supporting Ambedkar. Gandhi to Nehru to Patel—almost all the senior leaders of the Congress had demonstrated strong reservations about Ambedkar for one reason or the other. Ambedkar too never hid his aversion for the Congress and its leadership.

Gandhi and Ambedkar had profound disagreements. Even in 1955, seven years after Gandhi's death, Ambedkar would argue in a BBC interview that Gandhi was no 'Mahatma', not even 'from the point of view of his morality'. Gandhi too conveyed his reservations over Ambedkar's views in 1946 in a letter to Sardar Patel. 'One has to be very careful indeed' in dealing with Ambedkar, Gandhi cautioned.

Gandhi's ideological differences with Ambedkar date back to the Second Round Table Conference in 1932 when the British agreed to Ambedkar's proposal of separate electorates for Dalits. Gandhi went on a hunger strike forcing Ambedkar to the negotiating table, which resulted in the famous Poona Pact in December of that year. But Gandhi never hated Ambedkar. On the contrary, he invited Ambedkar to write his views in the *Harijan* in early 1933. Ambedkar argued in that article that 'there will be outcastes as long as there are castes' and said that 'nothing can help to save Hindus and ensure their survival in

[8]'Obituary Reference—Demise Of Dr. B. R. Ambedkar', *Parliament of India: Official Debates of Rajya Sabha*, http://tinyurl.com/36dryz7c. Accessed on 8 December 2024.

the coming struggle except the purging of the Hindu faith of this odious and vicious dogma.'[9]

When Nehru was unwilling to accommodate Ambedkar in the interim government in 1946, Gandhi, at the prodding of a young Dalit leader of the Congress, Jagjivan Ram, intervened to get him in. But that did not help Ambedkar much as Nehru and other leaders in the Congress never displayed any empathy. Ambedkar wrote in his resignation letter from the Cabinet in 1951 about the ill-treatment meted out to him by Nehru. In fact, Congress leaders did not make way for Ambedkar in the 1946 election from Mumbai. His Scheduled Castes Federation (SCF) was roundly defeated by Congress candidates. Jogendranath Mandal, an SCF leader from Bengal, came to Ambedkar's rescue and got him elected from Bengal with the Muslim League's help.

In the Constituent Assembly, Ambedkar found it tough to pursue his agenda for Hindu social reform and the upliftment of the scheduled castes. At one point, Sardar Patel told the 'Scheduled Caste friends' to 'forget what Ambedkar has done.'[10] Ambedkar's life-long desire to reform Hindu society through the Hindu Code Bill was blocked by the Congress at every stage, from the Constituent Assembly to Parliament, after 1950.

After Independence, the Congress leadership allowed the memory of Ambedkar to fade away until it was resurrected by Kanshi Ram in the 1980s through the Dalit Shoshit Samaj Sangharsh Samiti movement. None of the Congress governments in the first 40 years thought it prudent to offer Ambedkar a place of honour, prompting his grandson Prakash Ambedkar to accuse them of 'failing to do justice' to him. It was only in 1990

---

[9]'Dr. Ambedkar & Caste', *Bombay Sarvodaya Mandal & Gandhi Research Foundation*, http://tinyurl.com/yuet9bz4. Accessed on 8 January 2024.

[10]*Constituent Assembly Debates, Official Report, Vol. 5,* Lok Sabha Secretariat, New Delhi, 2014, http://tinyurl.com/5sks39v9. Accessed on 8 January 2024.

that the United Front government supported by the Bharatiya Janata Party honoured him with the Bharat Ratna.

On the other hand, Ambedkar maintained cordial relations with Hindutva icons whom Rahul Gandhi detests, like Savarkar and Swami Shraddhanand. In a letter to Savarkar, Ambedkar conveyed his 'appreciation of the work you are doing in the field of social reform'. In a special issue of his *Janata* magazine in April 1933, Ambedkar heaped praise on Savarkar saying that his contribution to the Dalit cause was as decisive and great as that of Gautama Buddha himself.[11]

Interestingly, Ambedkar was one of the first to use the word 'Hindutva'. In a statement issued in 1927 on the issue of temple entry, Ambedkar said, 'Hindutva belongs as much to the untouchable Hindus as to the touchable Hindus. To the growth and glory of this Hindutva, contributions have been made by Untouchables'.[12]

Ambedkar and Savarkar were opposed to religious orthodoxy among Hindus, whereas that orthodoxy was upheld by some of the Congress leaders of those times. It is important for Congress leaders to understand this history to learn who backstabbed whom.

They should also understand that when more than a lakh RSS volunteers fought against the draconian Emergency imposed by Indira Gandhi in 1975–77, they were protecting the dignity of the Indian Constitution, and when Mohan Bhagwat called the caste system as a thing of the past, he was resolutely pursuing Ambedkar's agenda.

Reprinted from THE INDIAN EXPRESS, with permission of The Indian Express (P) Limited.

---

[11]Keer, Dhananjay, *Veer Savarkar*, Popular Prakashan, 1950.

[12]Keer, Dhananjay, *Dr. Ambedkar: Life and Mission*, Popular Prakashan, 1954.

15

The Road to Constituent Assembly

Daniel Patrick Moynihan, the US senator who also served as ambassador to India in the 1970s, once made a profound remark that 'everyone is entitled to his own opinion, but not to his own facts'. Unfortunately, most of us do precisely that, especially while talking about history.

We must guard against this expediency of vilifying leaders—from Savarkar to those from the Sangh, Gandhi to Nehru and Bose to Ambedkar—based on a warped understanding of history. All those leaders fought the most difficult battles at the most daunting times and each made significant contributions in their own way. There could be disagreements over their ideological positions on different issues, whether it is Savarkar's dogged Hindutva or Nehru's dogmatic secularism. But that need not demean their other significant contributions.

India's freedom movement had seen many challenges, the most important of them being the process of securing an independent Constitution for it. In the immediate aftermath of the War of Independence in 1857, the British realized that the way to perpetuate their rule in the colony was by creating a rift between the Hindus and Muslims. *Divide et Impera* or Divide and Rule—the old Roman motto 'should be ours now', proclaimed Lord Mountstuart Elphinstone, who served as the governor of Bombay.

The British had worked on Muslim leaders like Syed Ahmad Khan and Aga Khan initially and settled for Muhammad Ali Jinnah in the end. Theodore Beck, a staunch imperialist, became the first principal of Syed Ahmad's Muhammadan Anglo-Oriental College (which became the Aligarh Muslim University later).[13] He once resorted to threats to the Muslim community saying that 'your ancestors were ruined because they opposed the government during the Mutiny... you are still suspects. Therefore, adopt loyalty... You are in a weak position, like a pumpkin. You should therefore be aware of the government's knife. Your life depends on the special concessions granted by the authorities. Therefore, you should always request them to safeguard your rights.'[14]

Aga Khan III was used by the British to establish the All-India Muslim League in 1906 as a counterweight to the fledgling nationalist movement led by the Indian National Congress. Lady Mary Minto, wife of Viceroy Lord Minto, recorded in her diary after the meeting between the members of the League and the viceroy in Shimla in 1906 that 'a very big thing has happened today. A work of statesmanship that will affect India and Indian history for many a long year. It is nothing less than the pulling back of 62 million people from joining the ranks of the seditious opposition.'

Finally, they turned to Jinnah to continue this tirade against the nationalist forces, which ended in the tragic partition of the country and the creation of Pakistan.

However, the British were well aware that it was impossible for them to rule over 300 million natives with the help of

---

[13]Siddiqui, Mohammad, 'Mr. Theodore Beck & Aligarh Muslim University', *Tawarikh Khwani*, 14 September 2020, http://tinyurl.com/3x8ue7vv. Accessed on 27 December 2023.

[14]Belmekki, Belkacem, *Sir Sayyid Ahmad Khan and the Muslim Cause in British India*, De Gruyter, 2010.

an army of about a 100,000. They realized that some form of a representative government formed through a constitutional route was necessary even for their own continuance. They had the experience of other colonies like Australia and Canada, where they imposed a constitutional government whose reins remained in the hands of the rulers in London. It was this model—something like a dominion status—that the British had offered to the leaders of the nationalist movement.

The leadership of the Indian National Congress was sandwiched between the two evils—the Muslim League separatism on one hand, and the British insistence on a dominion status on the other. The Congress leaders dithered on the first, but on the second challenge, they showed a remarkable sense of firmness. In retrospect, while the strategic blunder of competing appeasement of the Muslim League indulged in by the Congress leadership had resulted in the partition of the country, their steadfast opposition to the machinations of the British had led to India getting its own constitutional republic.

Its significance could be better understood by looking at the plight of other colonies like Australia. The British were rattled by the War of Independence of 1857 and decided to impose their parliamentary control over the Indian people. The Government of India Act of 1858, promulgated by the government of Lord Palmerston, abolished the rule of the East India Company in India and replaced it with Her Majesty's rule led by a member of the British cabinet as secretary of state for India assisted by a number of officials. No Indians were involved in that process.

The Indian experience also prompted the British to establish similar controls over all its colonies. They passed the Commonwealth of Australia Constitution Act of 1900, which came into effect on 1 January 1901. Under this Act, all the powers of the Australian government were vested in the British parliament and the British monarch became the monarch of Australia. It took 30 years for the Australian leaders to force the British to allow Australia to be represented at the international forums by Australians and another 50 years to curtail the powers of the British parliament to make laws for Australia. The Australia Act in 1986 finally ended the control of the British parliament over Australia.

However, the dominion status technically continues to this day with Australia, New Zealand and Canada still having the British monarch as their monarch. The issue was raked up several times in those countries, after the demise of Queen Victoria. Three judges of the Australian high court had opined earlier that the change of monarch in the UK need not automatically apply to its Commonwealth constituents. However, that constitutional status continues.

India would have been in a similar situation today had the British had their way. Fortunately, the Indian nationalist leadership was aware of the colonial designs and steadfastly resisted such attempt.

During World War I, when the British statesmen were haranguing about self-determination for all nations and people, some Indian leaders demanded that India be given the opportunity to draft a constitution for itself through the popularly elected representatives. However, for all their big talk about the self-determination of the nations, the British simply ignored the demand and declared through the Government of India Act of 1919 that 'each advance for the welfare and advancement of the Indian people' can be determined 'only by the [British] parliament.'

Indian nationalists were unhappy. Gandhi wrote that whenever Swaraj comes, it shall be through the will of the Indian people and the British parliament shall merely have the duty of ratifying their wishes. The demand for allowing the Indian legislature to draft its own Constitution gathered momentum after the Swaraj Party, the parliamentary wing of the Indian National Congress raised the issue inside the Legislative Assembly in 1924.

Instead of giving a sympathetic ear to the Indian demand, Secretary of State for India, Lord Birkenhead, in a speech in the House of Lords on 7 July 1925, challenged Indian leaders to 'produce a Constitution which carries behind it a fair measure of general agreement among the great people of India.' The British plan was simple. As long as the Muslim League and Jinnah were pitted against Congress, no Constitution could be possible. Hindu–Muslim tensions were at their peak during 1926–27. Taking advantage of this situation, Lord Birkenhead continued to taunt the Indian nationalist leadership until the appointment of the Simon Commission to look into the constitutional measures needed for India.

This time, the Congress leadership took up the gauntlet and appointed a committee led by Motilal Nehru in 1928. The committee produced its report. However, Birkenhead insisted that a general agreement of the political establishment was needed. The Congress leaders called an All Parties Conference to press for the Nehru Report to be ratified. As expected, the Muslim League and a few others opposed it and the initiative fell through. But Congress persisted with its demand that any Constitution for India would be drafted only through the popular will, and not through the British parliament route.

Meanwhile, after the third Round Table Conference, the British had come out with a White Paper in March 1933, which provided a scheme for the making of the Indian Constitution almost on similar lines as Australia. It was proposed that the provincial and federal governments will be provided with limited powers, while the viceroy, as His Majesty's representative, shall retain control over the army and foreign affairs, in addition to the power to reject any proposals that were found detrimental to any of the constitutional principles.

The Congress was quick to reject it. At a conference held in May 1934, the Swaraj Party passed a resolution against the White Paper. 'Proposals of His Majesty's Government for the new Constitution of the Government of India contained in the White Paper are considered as a whole not only a negation of the National Demand made by Mr Gandhi on behalf of the Congress at the Second RTC and calculated to perpetuate the political subjection and economic exploitation of the Indian people (sic),' it thundered. The conference reiterated that the only course should be to convene a Constituent Assembly representing all sections of the Indian people to frame an 'acceptable Constitution'.

This was the first time that the Indian masses heard about the demand for a Constituent Assembly. Meanwhile, the British, ignoring Congress' demand, went ahead and promulgated the Government of India Act of 1935. The Act provided for the formation of elected assemblies at the federal and provincial levels, leaving the Congress in a dilemma. Finally, in December 1936, it declared through a resolution its 'entire rejection' of the Government of India Act and the 'Constitution that has been imposed on India'. However, boycotting the elections for provincial and national legislatures was not seen as a wise option. Hence, the Congress declared that it 'repeats its resolve not to submit to this Constitution or to cooperate with it, but to combat it, both inside and outside the legislatures, so as to end it.'

When the British government sought Indian support in World War II, the Congress once again demanded a categorical commitment from them for the 'recognition of India's independence' and 'the right of her people to frame their Constitution through a Constituent Assembly.' Congress' demand was that the Constituent Assembly should be an elected body through the universal adult franchise, a principle that it had enunciated at the time of the Nehru Report in 1928.

Obviously, the British did not heed Congress' demand and went ahead with involving India in the war, resulting in the the Congress quitting all provincial governments where it was in power since the 1937 elections. The next seven years saw Congress waging battles both on the streets as well as on the constitutional front. While the battles on the streets were waged by many others, the Congress was alone in the constitutional battles. It also had to endure opposition from within the country.

Opposition to the popularly elected Constituent Assembly came from the Muslim League as expected. It argued that such an Assembly would be a Hindu-majority body. Jinnah demanded 50 per cent seats for Muslims in any such elected body. Pakistani-American historian Ayesha Jalal's 'sole spokesman' also insisted that all Muslims would be nominated only by the League.

Besides the Muslim League, moderates in Congress, too, had apprehensions about the wisdom of involving ordinary 'illiterate' people in the process of drafting the Constitution. They, instead, suggested the route of a round table conference of parties and eminences. More vehement opposition came from the princes and landlords, who owed their power and position to British paramountcy. Nehru's insistence on a popularly elected Constituent Assembly, Gandhi's suggestion that minorities would get proper representation and Rajagopalachari's statement that princes were not minorities, and hence their states will be treated on par with the British provinces caused consternation in the royal courts about their own future.

As the tussle continued, the Cabinet Mission, led by Sir

Pethick-Lawrence, Sir Stafford Cripps and A.V. Alexander, came to India in 1946. Clement Attlee, the then prime minister (PM) of Britain, mandated the mission to work out modalities for the transfer of power in India. Under the Cabinet Mission Plan, Viceroy Wavell appointed a government led by Jawaharlal Nehru in 1946.

A Constituent Assembly was elected in December 1946 with 389 members. Although leaders like Gandhi and Nehru always insisted that it would be a popularly elected body, given the turbulent times, it was formed through an indirect route by the election of members by provincial assemblies. More than a dozen big princely states, which were willing to join the Indian dominion, also nominated their members. Muslim League, however, boycotted it.

Finally, after the return of the Cabinet Mission, PM Attlee made the important announcement about the Indian Independence Act 1947, in February of that year, which secured royal assent in July after it was accepted by both the Congress and the Muslim League on 3 June. This Act had vindicated Congress' stand by formally acceding that the British parliament would have no power whatsoever over law-making in India once the country was granted independence. That included the period of close to 30 months after Independence, during which the country remained a dominion.

The Constitution-making process, led by B.R. Ambedkar, went on for two years, 11 months and 18 days, and the final draft was presented to the nation on 26 November 1949. It was signed by all members on 24 January 1950, and became the Constitution of India two days later on 26 January 1950.

It was a significant achievement in the sense that unlike the other colonies, our Constitution did not allow any semblance of colonial control. But did it achieve all the hoary ideals that leaders like Gandhi and Nehru articulated?

'A Constituent Assembly... does not mean a body of people, or a gathering of able lawyers, who are intent on drawing up a Constitution. It means a nation on the move, throwing away the shell of its past political and possibly social structure, and fashioning for itself a new garment of its own making. It means the masses of a country in action through their elected representatives,' Nehru wrote.

The Constituent Assembly lived up to all those ideals, although a majority of its members were lawyers.

Reprinted from OPEN MAGAZINE, with permission of Open Media Network Pvt. Ltd.

16

J&K's Accession Pact with India

History serves the masters of the past. But historians serve the masters of the present too. That's why Napoleon quipped that history is, after all, a 'fable, mutually agreed upon'.

The accession of the princely state of Jammu and Kashmir (J&K) into the Indian Union in October 1947 became a subject of fabled scrutiny. It may be useful to look at it from the prism of some authentic sources.

There are a few accurate first-hand accounts of the last years of India's freedom movement in books such as *The Transfer of Power in India* by V.P. Menon, *The Great Divide* by H.V. Hodson and *Mission with Mountbatten* by Alan Campbell Johnson. Menon, as secretary to Home Minister Vallabhbhai Patel, was a party to the events of that period, and Johnson served as Mountbatten's press attaché. Their accounts tell us that none of the Indian leaders were prepared to leave J&K to Pakistan. The state had 'the greatest strategic value, perhaps, in all India', Mahatma Gandhi emphasized.

That the Indian leaders were keen on not letting Kashmir go to Pakistan became clear when they managed to divide Gurdaspur district and secure two-thirds of it to East Punjab. Gurdaspur was the critical land link to Kashmir. It had a marginal Muslim majority of 51.2 per cent. Muhammad Ali Jinnah was confident that the district would become a part of Pakistan, and consequently, the Maharaja of Kashmir would be left with no choice but to join him. But Jawaharlal Nehru and Patel determinedly prevailed upon the British to avert that eventuality.

That paved the way for the accession of Kashmir to India, about which several myths exist. Patel, ably assisted by Menon, was able to persuade most of the princely states to join the Dominion of India. However, it was not just Kashmir, Junagadh and Hyderabad, which remained troublesome, but at least another 15 princes remained troublesome, the most prominent among them being the ruler of Jodhpur. It was the Mountbatten-Menon duo that played hardball, with the viceroy warning the Maharaja of Jodhpur that his decision to join Pakistan would 'surely be in conflict with the principle underlying the partition of India', and lead to 'serious communal trouble inside the state'. The Maharaja finally signed the accession papers on 11 August, not before pulling out his revolver to threaten to kill Menon.

The Maharaja of Kashmir continued to dither. His strained relations with Nehru were a big impediment. In fact, in 1946, he got Nehru arrested when the latter visited Srinagar to support Sheikh Abdullah's movement. This personal rivalry, together with the urge to remain independent, must have prompted the Maharaja to procrastinate on the question of accession.

Efforts to convince the Maharaja began in May 1947 with J.B. Kriplani visiting Srinagar. Patel also deployed rulers from Patiala, Kapurthala, Faridkot and some hill states to persuade him. But all those efforts failed.

Mountbatten himself went to Kashmir on 17–23 June. Before going, he sought a note from Nehru. In a long note, Nehru made a strong pitch for Kashmir's accession to India. He also asked Mountbatten to press for the removal of Ram

Chandra Kak as prime minister (PM) and the release of Sheikh Abdullah. 'The normal and obvious course appears to be for Kashmir to join the Constituent Assembly of India,' Nehru insisted in that note. Mountbatten's mission too failed.

Gandhi once again asked Mountbatten if he could go. Nehru betrayed restlessness by writing to Mountbatten on 27 July that although he was busy with many things in Delhi, he would still want to go 'as Kashmir has become first priority with me'. But the Maharaja was categorical that the visit of the Indian leaders would disturb the peace in his state. Mountbatten found Nehru's insistence on a visit to Srinagar when 'Kak and Maharaja hate him' to be preposterous. He added, 'I had visions of Maharaja declaring adherence to Pakistan just before Nehru arrived and Kak provoking an incident which would end up by Nehru being arrested.' Finally, Patel intervened and Gandhi was allowed to visit the state in the first week of August.

Gandhi's visit brought some hope as Kak resigned as PM on 11 August and the Maharaja opened negotiations with the Congress leadership. He also set Sheikh Abdullah free later that month and invited him for consultations. His army started tackling pro-Pakistan elements in the state sternly. Yet, a final decision eluded.

Nehru kept reminding Patel about the urgency of accession. He would hop across the street from his house to Patel's to alert him about the approaching winter which 'would cut off Kashmir from rest of India' and allow Pakistan to go ahead 'without much fear of consequences, specially when the winter isolates Kashmir'.

In October, a defence committee was formed with Mountbatten as chairman and Nehru, Patel, Gopalaswamy Ayyangar and others as members. Sardar prevailed upon the Maharaja, resulting in the appointment of Mehr Chand Mahajan as the new PM on 15 October.

Meanwhile, Jinnah made the fatal mistake of invading Kashmir on 22 October using armed tribesmen. India moved quickly by sending Menon to Srinagar on 25 October with a promise of army assistance and the Maharaja handed over his signed accession papers to Menon that evening before moving to a safer Jammu. The rest is history.

17

The Tricolour in Kashmir

Gupkaris sound dubious sometimes. The senior leader Farooq Abdullah had stirred a hornet's nest by hinting that the Kashmiris were looking at China as their redeemer. Insisting that China 'never accepted' the revocation of Article 370, Farooq told *India Today* that 'They (the Chinese) said till you restore Article 370, we won't stop'. Leaders of his party and the Gupkar group attempted a feeble defence by claiming that he only made a matter-of-fact statement but never invited China to support the Kashmiris. Yet, his hasty statement led to further stereotyping of the Kashmiri leaders as 'anti-nationals'.

Denials apart, Abdullah appeared to be carried away by the street-side talk about China in the valley. There is a widely circulated myth among the Kashmiris about a breed of people—Yajuj and Majuj—who broadly fit the description of the Chinese. Those mythical people were supposed to be invincible because of their sheer numbers. If they get after somebody, he is doomed by the sheer nuisance they cause. The separatist circles in Kashmir are agog with the whispers that the Chinese (a la yojujg and mojujg) have gotten after India and will make life miserable for it. It is even seen as a divine intercession to help the Kashmiris. It is intriguing that a leader of Farooq Abdullah's stature could be influenced by such separatist fake myths.

Mehbooba Mufti, the other senior leader of the group, held a press conference to dare the Indian state that she would not hold up the Indian flag until the Jammu and Kashmir (J&K) flag has been restored. '*Jo haath 35A ke saath ched chaad karne ke liye uthenge, wo haath hi nahi wo saara jism jal ke raakh ho jaega* (Not only the hand, which will raise to tamper with 35A, but the whole body will burn to ashes),' she once reportedly threatened at a party meeting. When the Articles 370 and 35A were revoked by the Indian Parliament, she argued that there would not be a single Kashmiri left to uphold the national Tricolor in the valley. Ironically, one year down the line, while the national flag flutters in many hands, she remained the only person to hold up the Kashmiri flag, displaying it on the table during that press conference.

Kashmiri leaders are prone to such provocations and subsequent somersaults. The popular caricature in Kashmir about Sheik Abdullah was that he would be a separatist in the Valley, regionalist in Jammu and a nationalist in Delhi. Farooq Abdullah too inherited it. He would sing Ram *dhun* (tune) in Delhi and separatist dhun in Srinagar. Mehbooba is no exception either. She can be her rhetorical best in hard-line harangue on the valley streets. But just a couple of years ago at a party convention, she was also heard telling her partymen that 'If there is anyone with the mandate to heal the wounds of people of Jammu and Kashmir, take the state out of the morass, it is only Narendra Modiji and no one else'. A senior Kashmir leader pointedly told her about the hollowness of her national flag rhetoric. The national flag was not just a piece of cloth; he reprimanded her, reminding that it is in the official bungalow that she lives in, the official bulletproof car that she travels by and the security cover that she enjoys.

It is no surprise that the Gupkar leaders face a major credibility challenge in the eyes of the people of Kashmir.

Their continued rhetoric about revocation of Articles 370 and 35A and the accompanying hard-line statements are meant only to mislead the innocent Kashmiris. History is witness to the campaign in 1950s and 60s by Sheik Abdullah and others about 'pre-1947 status'. But after the Delhi Agreement between Indira Gandhi and Sheik Abdullah in 1975, the goalpost was shifted to 'pre-1953 status'. Some Gupkar leaders now talk about restoration of statehood as the central issue, thus shifting the goalpost further to 'pre-2019 status'.

Reprinted from DECCAN HERALD, with permission of Printers (Mysore) Private Limited.

18

The Long-Due Recognition for Netaji

Rajpath, the 1911-vintage Kingsway built to welcome King George V, became Kartavya Path. A tall black-stone statue of Netaji Subhas Chandra Bose, described by Prime Minister (PM) Narendra Modi as the 'first Pradhan of united India', was installed under the canopy where King George V's statue stood. This is New India's final push for dismantling colonial-era remnants. At the unveiling function, PM Modi described Rajpath as a symbol of slavery and hoped that Kartavya Path would motivate people's representatives toward India's 'democratic past and universal ideals'.

India's Independence movement was inspired not just by the desire to replace the British with Indian rulers but by the passion to return to its civilizational glory. Lala Lajpat Rai, Madan Mohan Malaviya, Bal Gangadhar Tilak, V.D. Savarkar, Sri Aurobindo and M.K. Gandhi—many leaders were committed to that ideal. Even Jawaharlal Nehru, the Cambridge-educated young man whom Gandhi affectionately described once as 'our Englishman', was so determinedly anti-British that he threatened to resign from Congress in 1928 when the Nehru Committee, headed by his father Motilal Nehru, recommended that India may accept the British offer of dominion status. Nothing short of Purna Swaraj (complete independence), junior Nehru insisted.

Sadly though, those motivations waned when Independence dawned. In 1948, India decided to join the so-called Commonwealth. Most of these Commonwealth countries have nothing in common except their colonial past—nor any wealth—yet India continues to be a member. The silver lining is that unlike countries like Canada, Australia and New Zealand, India did not remain under British dominion after Independence.

Some half-hearted efforts were made after Independence to remove the symbols of colonialism. Names of some roads and buildings were changed. But the statue of King George V remained on Rajpath for a full two decades until a public agitation forced the government in 1968 to shift it to another venue. The canopy remained empty because the leadership was undecided over who should occupy it. Gandhi's name was proposed several times but turned down during the regimes of Indira Gandhi and Rajiv Gandhi.

Prime Minister Modi is giving a new thrust to that effort. The new parliament building, Kartavya Path, National War Memorial and the statue of Netaji are all the new symbols of a decolonizing India.

Some found the installation of Netaji's statue on Kartavya Path less convincing. India's identity from its Independence was that of non-violence, they argue. It is precisely that narrative which needs to change. India's independence movement had many strands, the non-violent one led by Gandhi being the most prominent. But Netaji's contribution was no less significant.

In fact, Netaji's Azad Hind Fauj or Indian National Army (INA) had hit the last nail in the British coffin in the penultimate years of the Independence struggle. Netaji's scintillating address at a rally in Burma, in which he gave the thunderous appeal, 'Give me blood and I promise you freedom', led to a tectonic shift in that struggle.

Indian National Army's adventurous battles and the capture of Moirang in Manipur under the leadership of Lt Col Shaukat Ali Malik on 14 April 1944 had triggered a wave of enthusiasm among the masses of India, who were disappointed by the failure of the Quit India movement. This enthusiasm turned into anger when the British brought 11 INA soldiers to Red Fort for a trial in 1945. The fire lit by the INA was so fierce that rebellions broke out in the Royal Indian Navy with Indian soldiers, who constituted the majority in the force, refusing to obey the orders of their British officers.

The rebels, who started calling themselves the Indian National Navy on the lines of Netaji's INA, mutinied initially at Bombay in 1946, but the unrest soon spread from Karachi to Calcutta. It involved over 20,000 sailors and 78 ships. At the peak of the revolt, sections of the Royal Indian Air Force and Royal Indian Army too joined the revolt. There were incidents of unrest in the army cantonments of Madras and Poona. The Indian soldiers started defying their British superiors and saluting with their left hand as a mark of revolt.

Although ideologically opposed to violent struggles, the Indian National Congress leadership too saw in the INA trials of an opportunity to reignite the spirit of freedom among the masses and came forward to defend the INA soldiers. The defence team deployed by the Congress included prominent legal luminaries like Bhulabhai Desai, Asaf Ali, Sarat Chandra Bose, Tej Bahadur Sapru, Kailash Nath Katju and Lt Col Horilal Varma. Even Jawaharlal Nehru scrambled for the black coat that he relinquished in 1922 and jumped to the defence of the INA soldiers at the Red Fort.

The British were rattled by these revolts and the massive popular support they received. Debates in the British House of Commons in the second half of 1946 stand testimony to it.

Prime Minister Clement Atlee decided that it was time to quit India. He gave two principal reasons for his decision: one, that the Indian soldiers of the Royal Indian Army were no longer loyal to the crown, and second, the British Army could no longer afford to send a large contingent of British soldiers to India, especially after the bloody experience of World War II.

Netaji's and INA's contribution to the Independence struggle thus becomes no less important than that of Gandhi and Congress. The Modi government has used Amrit Mahotsav to accord appropriate recognition to that and many such contributions. A grateful nation should cherish the memories of all those great freedom fighters.

It is important to remember that all contributions were great. Nehru would not become small by making Patel big; Gandhi would not be dwarfed by making Netaji prominent. In their lifetime, those leaders had probably disagreed but never hated each other. In fact, it was Netaji who gave Gandhi the title of 'Father of the Nation' in a message from Burma in 1944 on his seventy-fifth birthday. Why then should we politicize Modi's sincere efforts to accord a place of glory to all the freedom fighters?

19

The Significance of 26 January

'Why 26 January?'—We never ask this question. The final draft of the Indian constitution was passed by the Constituent Assembly on 26 November 1949 after Rajendra Prasad, chairman of the Assembly, delivered his final address. On 25 November, B.R. Ambedkar had laid the final draft of the Constitution with an insightful address. Then why did the nation wait for two full months before accepting the Constitution and converting India from a dominion to a republic?

There was a twenty-year saga behind it which not many people know. Self-governance to India was a demand put forth by the Indian National Congress after Mahatma Gandhi's ascendance. Towards that, certain constitutional reforms were demanded from the British. There existed two streams in Congress during that period—moderates and extremists. The extremists demanded 'total independence' from the British, while the moderates were willing to work under the British paramountcy.

Interestingly, Gandhi was on the side of the moderates while Jawaharlal Nehru, who had returned from Europe in 1927 after attending the decennial celebrations of the Soviet Russian government as a committed socialist, sided with the extremists and demanded that the British Raj should end forthwith. At the Madras Congress session in 1927, Nehru got a resolution passed declaring Congress's goal as 'complete national independence.' Gandhi was not impressed at all. Six years earlier, at the Nagpur Congress session, too, Gandhi rejected the proposal for Purna Swaraj (complete independence), mooted by leaders like Keshav Baliram Hedgewar.

This time, Gandhi vented his anger saying: 'The Congress stultified itself by repeating year after year resolutions of this character when it knows that it is not capable of carrying them into effect. By passing such resolutions, we make an exhibition of our impotence. We have almost sunk to the level of schoolboys' debating society,' he chided Nehru and others.

The Simon Commission was to visit India in 1928 to discuss the constitutional reforms for self-government. The Congress leadership was opposed to it on the ground that there was not a single Indian member in the Commission. Moreover, its proposal to grant dominion status to India was not acceptable to the extremists in Congress. As a result, the Commission had faced protests wherever it went. Enraged, the Commission taunted Congress to come up with its own Constitution. Not to be cowed down, the leadership had accepted that challenge and formed an All Parties Conference under the leadership of Motilal Nehru for that task. The draft of the Constitution was soon ready in which it was categorically stated that—'Every person of either sex who has attained the age of 21, and is not disqualified by law, shall be entitled to vote.'

However, that draft, known as Nehru Report after its chairman, Motilal Nehru, had acceded to dominion status to the chagrin of many extremists in Congress, including Jawaharlal Nehru. A year's time was given to the British government to accept the Nehru Report, failing which, Congress had the option of returning to its demand of Purna Swaraj.

Viceroy Lord Irwin plunged into action to press London

to accede to the dominion status for India. A round table conference of Indian leaders was called in London to discuss dominion status and draft a constitution. Nehru and Subhas Chandra Bose, two leaders of the Garam Dal—the extremist section of Congress—resigned from the Working Committee protesting dominion status. After Gandhi entered into an agreement with Viceroy Irwin, known as the Gandhi–Irwin Pact, under which several concessions were given to Congress, the extremist leaders were persuaded to withdraw their resignations and return to the Working Committee.

In 1929, the annual Congress session was held in Lahore under the presidentship of Jawaharlal Nehru. Purna Swaraj was once again declared as the sole objective of the Congress. All-out war was declared against the British in the name of the civil disobedience programme. As a first step, all the Congress legislators in provinces and at the Centre were asked to step down. 178 of them had immediately responded by resigning.

26 January 1930 was declared 'Independence Day' and a call was given to celebrate it nationwide. Thousands of meetings were held across the country on that day. A solemn pledge was taken by lakhs of people, which said: 'It is the inalienable right of the Indian people, as of any other people, to have freedom and to enjoy the fruits of their toil.' It further said: 'If any government deprives a people of these rights and oppresses them, they have a further right to alter it or abolish it.'

Later, at the Karachi session in 1931, the Congress had passed a resolution on 'fundamental rights.' Described as 'a minimum programme' for Congress, it guaranteed such freedoms like expression, religion, thought and assembly; equality before law irrespective of sex, creed or caste; protection to regional languages and cultures; minimum living wages, limited hours of work and old-age insurance for industrial workers; safeguards against unemployment; abolition of untouchability; universal adult franchise; free primary education; prohibition; state control and management of key industries and services; and most importantly, the establishment of a secular state. After a few years, in 1937, Nehru formed various committees of experts to work on India's planning. Out of that emerged the National Planning Committee with Nehru as its chairman. A planned economy, the socialist model, was thus set in motion by Nehru, 10 years before the Independence of the country.

It was in remembrance of 26 January 1930 that Nehru had chosen 26 January 1950 as Republic Day. While that day finally ended the three-year dominion status of India and transformed it into a full-fledged republic, many of the aspects of the two-decades-old 'minimum programme', too, found a place in the Constitution of India adopted on that day. A Planning Commission, with Nehru as the chairman and P.C. Mahalanobis, a statistician as its key member, also came into being almost simultaneously.

Interestingly, the 20-year hiatus was not without events. The Naram Dal and Garam Dal (moderates and extremists) continued to battle it out through various stages of the freedom movement during that period. Gandhi, who did not live to see the country turning a republic in 1950, was there trying to play the role of the balancer during those eventful years of the run-up to India's freedom. He was not always too pleased with Nehru's aggression and impatience. 'Differences between you and me appear to be so vast and so radical that there seems to be no meeting ground between us,' he told Nehru on one occasion. On his part, Nehru, too, had openly lashed out at Gandhi on more than one occasion conveying his disagreement in a youthful manner. But in the end, the two never truly broke up. 'No amount of political differences will ever separate him from me,' Gandhi told Patel once.

26 January 1930 was Nehru's triumph over the moderates

like Tej Bahadur Sapru and M.R. Jayakar. His own father Motilal, too, was moderate, but he did not live long after the Nehru Report. Subhas Chandra Bose was on Jawaharlal Nehru's side in 1930. Sardar Patel began on friendly terms with Nehru as the latter fully supported him during the Bardoli Satyagraha in 1928, which was in a way the beginning of Patel's Congress career, but soon grew disillusioned with Nehru's radical ideological moorings. So were other seniors like Rajendra Prasad and Jamnalal Bajaj. At one point in 1936, six senior leaders, including Rajendra Prasad, Sardar Patel and C. Rajagopalachari, had resigned from the Congress Working Committee protesting the 'preaching and emphasising of socialism' by Nehru who was the Congress president at that time. Nehru countered their resignation with the threat of his own resignation. Gandhi, as usual, intervened to pacify both groups.

Nehru and Patel hardly got along during those two decades, but Patel for one, as an elderly statesman, never allowed his differences to overshadow the larger Congress mission. And there was Gandhi, always trying to convince the fellow Gujarati to step back and allow the 'rightful helmsman of the Congress'—as he described Nehru—to move on with his agenda.

To his credit, Nehru was determined that India should at no cost agree to any subservient status under the British. Although he worked with his Congress colleagues under various programmes devised by the British, he never gave up his goal of 'complete independence'. He also dismissed the Government of India Act of 1935 as a 'slave Constitution'. Although forced by his colleagues to join the Viceroy Wavell's Executive Council in 1946, he never showed any enthusiasm. When the naval mutiny broke out at Bombay and Karachi, Nehru openly supported the mutineers calling them a 'fine body of young men'. When the trial of the Indian National Army (INA) began at the Red Fort, Nehru was there in defence of the INA, wearing the long-discarded lawyers' robe once again.

When the Cabinet Mission came to India in 1946 to initiate proceedings for Independence and the formation of the Constituent Assembly, Nehru was categorical that Congress would not be bound by any conditions, and the Constituent Assembly would function as a 'completely sovereign body'.

Finally, the Constituent Assembly met for the first time on 9 December 1946. With Muslim League boycotting it, the Assembly turned out as partitioned India's body. Moving the objectives resolution, Nehru declared that 'the first task of this Assembly is to free India through a new Constitution... and to give every Indian the fullest opportunity to develop himself according to his capacity. It is a resolution and yet it is something much more than a resolution. It is a declaration. It is a firm resolve. It is a pledge and an undertaking, and it is for all of us, I hope, a dedication,' he passionately proclaimed.

It was that dedication of 299 members who sat over 114 days spread over two years, 11 months and 18 days[15], that had resulted in the making of one of the world's largest and most comprehensive of constitutions.

Ambedkar, as the chairman of the Drafting Committee, delivered his final address on 25 November 1949. It remains one of his best oratories in history. His closing comments must continue to ring in our ears always:

> If we wish to preserve the Constitution in which we have sought to enshrine the principle of Government of the people, for the people and by the people, let us

[15]'Constitution Day', *mygov.in*, http://tinyurl.com/3smtt3sm. Accessed on 22 January 2024.

resolve not to be tardy in the recognition of the evils that lie across our path and which induce people to prefer Government for the people to Government by the people, nor to be weak in our initiative to remove them. That is the only way to serve the country. I know of no better.

Reprinted from OPEN MAGAZINE, with permission of Open Media Network Pvt. Ltd.

20

Sardar Patel and the Kashmir Question

Prime Minister (PM) Modi was not off the mark when he said, '…if Sardar Patel was the first PM of India there would not have been a Jammu and Kashmir problem.'

Napoleon once called history 'a fable mutually agreed upon'. What we call history is sometimes a popular myth that is politically and ideologically convenient. The history of accession of Jammu and Kashmir (J&K) to India is a classic case of this myth-making. A lot of haze surrounds the historic accession of the princely state that took place on 26 October 1947. That allows for leaders in Kashmir to repeat the myth of 'conditional accession'.

The final chapter in India's Independence saga was the challenge of the accession of the 565 princely states into one of the two dominions by 15 August 1947. A single document called the Instrument of Accession was to be the basis for the accession. It was the same accession document that the Maharaja of Kashmir signed too.

The National Conference, led by Sheikh Abdullah, held a special session in October 1948 to support the accession. It did not talk about any conditions. Supporting accession, it only said: 'This convention has given serious thought to the question of accession…After mature consideration it is definitely of the opinion that Kashmir cannot find its proper place in Pakistan, which today has become the main citadel of reaction and decaying feudalism.'

Three people—Louis Mountbatten, Sardar Vallabhbhai Patel and V.P. Menon—played a critical role in the political integration of India. The British government's political department was replaced with the 'states department' in May 1947 to facilitate the process. Patel was made the minister and Menon the administrative head. Although all three leaders played crucial roles in the integration of the states, Patel was rightfully credited with the epithet of iron man, on the lines of the German Iron Chancellor, Otto von Bismarck. Bismarck, a Prussian general, was responsible for the integration of German-speaking kingdoms into a united Germany in 1871. Bismarck was alone in his campaign, but the kingdoms he was uniting were smaller and largely city-states. Patel was assisted in the task by Mountbatten and Menon, but he faced a much tougher challenge as he had to deal with many big princely states with armies, assemblies and treasuries.

Mountbatten, entrusted by the Cabinet with the responsibility of accession, convened a meeting of the princes on 25 July 1947, and managed to secure the accession papers signed by almost all of them before 15 August 1947. The three princely states that refused to accede—Hyderabad, Junagadh and Kashmir—became Patel's responsibility. It is the final accession of these three, which Patel secured through various methods, that won him the title 'Bismarck of India'.

Compared to the accession of Hyderabad and Junagadh, where Patel had to use force or threat, Kashmir's case was more complicated. Jawaharlal Nehru's fondness for Sheikh Abdullah on the one hand, and Maharaja Hari Singh's ambition to remain independent on the other, made Patel's task difficult. Nehru and Patel wanted the Maharaja to build a friendship with

Abdullah while simultaneously acceding his state to the Indian dominion. The Maharaja dithered on both the counts, until the Pakistani tribesmen from Khyber Pakhtunkhwa invaded his state on 22 October 1947, and marched towards Srinagar. Mountbatten's conversations with Jinnah on 1 November 1947 revealed the involvement of Pakistan in the invasion.

The tribal invasion and Patel's persuasion finally led the Maharaja to hand over signed accession papers to Menon on 26 October 1947. Patel lost no time in sending the Indian army to Srinagar. By the end of the year, the invaders were pushed back across the Jhelum. Winter halted the progress of the operation. The Pakistan army arrived on the scene by the time the winter ended, forcing a stand-off between the two countries at what is described today as the Line of Control. Once the Pakistan army got involved, Nehru insisted that the issue became international and removed it from Patel's purview. The rest is a history of blunders, which the present government is seeking to ameliorate.

Patel continued with his unfinished agenda of the accession of Junagadh and Hyderabad. Junagadh came under the control of the Indian administration in November 1947, while Hyderabad needed a police action in September 1948 to fall in line. He ensured that in spite of the recalcitrant rulers and restive population, both Junagadh and Hyderabad integrated fully with India without any difficulty. But Kashmir, taken out of his purview, would fester for long.

Sardar Patel was a loyal disciple of Mahatma Gandhi. He was not ambitious. When Gandhi once asked him about his mission after Independence, Patel's reply was that he would become a sadhu. His modesty helped Nehru climb the political ladder easily. History does not have ifs and buts. Yet, PM Narendra Modi was not off the mark when he said in the Rajya Sabha in 2019, 'It is our belief that if Sardar Patel was the first PM of India there would not have been a Jammu and Kashmir problem.'

Reprinted from HINDUSTAN TIMES, with permission of HT Media Ltd.

21

Xi's Return to Mao's Coterie

When Xi Jinping rose to become the General Secretary of the Communist Party of China (CPC), some called him China's Mikhail Gorbachev. Many hoped that he would take forward the moderate policies of his predecessors, Jiang Zemin and Hu Jintao. From a Communist authoritarian dictatorship under Mao, the CPC had gradually transformed into a party with moderate views and a semblance of inner-party democracy and collective functioning under Xi's predecessors.

Coming after four general secretaries trained under Deng Xiaoping's liberal ideological wings, Xi Jinping was widely seen as someone who would further that agenda. 10 years later, when he rose before the National People's Congress seeking approval for the extension of his tenure, many would see in him not a Gorbachev but a combination of Mao and Stalin.

In the last decade, Xi has not only meticulously dismantled Deng's democratic moderation but also distanced himself from his father whose enormous goodwill was the main reason for Xi's rise. Like many others in the CPC, Xi too is a princeling—a derogatory term used in China for leaders who rise up the ranks due to nepotism and cronyism.

There is one difference though. Unlike the fathers of other princelings, Xi Jinping's illustrious father Xi Zhongxun is held in high esteem in China for his contributions during the revolution years and subsequently in building modern China. He was one of the key associates of Mao during the guerrilla struggles and served in many important positions after the revolution. Like Deng Xiaoping, Xi Zhongxun too held moderate views on the economy and faced the ire of Mao. He was purged from the party posts several times, imprisoned and condemned to hard labour after 1965.

Zongxun returned to the party along with Deng after Mao's death and became an important official in the National People's Congress. Xi Jinping, his second son, owes his rise hugely to his father. It was the blessings of the Deng-era old guard that ensured his elevation to the party's Central Committee in 2007 and subsequently to the post of general secretary.

Once in that position, Xi turned out to be the opposite of his father. Three decades after Mao's death, Xi brought back memories of the dreadful three decades of Mao's era. Mao built a party structure centred on his own personality. A coterie of sycophants controlled him. He whimsically ran the party affairs, often through hand-written slips sent to party meetings that would seal the fate of many leaders. Deng put an end to this personality cult and authoritarianism when he became the supreme leader in 1978. He nurtured a new generation of leaders like Hu Yaobang, Zhao Ziyang, Jiang Zemin and Hu Jintao—the four predecessors of Xi Jinping—who were committed to collective leadership and economic liberalism. Deng introduced limited democracy in the party in 1987 by allowing more candidates to run for the Congress than the number of posts. He also introduced the principle of two terms for the President.

While undoing that legacy, Xi has not only returned to Mao's coterie authoritarianism but also resorted to Stalin's ruthlessness. He has built a cruel surveillance state and purged tens of thousands of cadres at various levels on flimsy pretexts. The drive against corruption became a euphemism for neutralizing Xi's political rivals. Senior party leaders like Zhou Yongkang, a Standing Committee member; Sun Zhengcai; Bo Xilai and Politburo members were among the over 400 leaders who became victims of Xi's campaign in the last decade. The hypocrisy of the campaign is glaring. Xi's close friends, like Jia Qinglin, a Standing Committee member who was instrumental in Xi's rise, remain untouched despite serious charges of corruption.

Xi pounced upon dissent and curbed internet freedom. Critics like Cai Xia, who once taught at the Central Party School in Beijing, had to leave China or languish in jails. Xi used dazzling propaganda to hide his failures on the economic and pandemic front. He successfully installed his confidantes in the Standing Committee, a key body that can make or mar his chances for another term. Even in the Chinese Army, Xi affected brutal purges of officers seen as less loyal to him and installed his own loyalists in key positions.

Finally, there was growing resentment among the people over Xi's handling of the Covid-19 lockdowns, which caused enormous suffering to citizens. Chinese social media is replete with dark humour. One of the most circulated posts during the peak of the pandemic called for an urgent CPC meeting so that the country can get rid of the leaders. Xi faced a barrage of criticism when Nancy Pelosi called his bluff by landing in Taipei.

But Xi was in no mood to budge. Hyper-nationalism is his weapon. He took on America and proclaimed that China was 'invincible'. He is raring for war with Taiwan, which could unleash forces that would either decimate his leadership or push the world into a horrendous conflict.

Either way, the world should brace itself for a Chinese winter that could heat up.

22

Reviving Jinnah's Politics

Debate over civic and cultural nationalism is at least a century old. Hans Kohn, an eminent American historian of nationalism, was the first to raise this dichotomy, influencing the Western studies on nationalism in a big way. Kohn argued that national identities in the Ancient Greek and Jewish societies were developed around certain cultural traits like 'the idea of the chosen people, the emphasis on a common history and future, national messianism, and the supreme loyalty to political community'. In his view, the Enlightenment era in Europe had led to a major transformation, paving the way for formation of nation states based on the concept of civic or constitutional nationalism.

Kohn's major works were published around the time of World War II. Scholars misinterpreted Hitler and Mussolini's fascism as 'nationalist excesses'. Kohn's views were immediately lapped up without proper scrutiny. Cultural nationalism was dismissed as Hitlerian and fascist, and a clamour for the ill-defined civic nationalism came to dominate the discourse.

Hitler was not a nationalist—neither cultural nor civic. He was a race supremacist with an imperialist mindset. The 'Third Reich' he talked about was modelled on the 'First Reich', which was the German Holy Roman empire. In his autobiography, *Mein Kampf* (My Story), Hitler explicitly rejects national identities as 'misbegotten monstrosities', and declares his mission as 'preservation and advancement of a community of physically and psychically homogeneous creatures' by 'assembling and preserving the most valuable stocks of basic racial elements'. He wanted to raise this race to a 'dominant position' until it became a 'master people' and 'mistress of the globe'.

Kohn's civic nationalism argument came under scrutiny of many academics later for its oversimplification of the nationalism question. A healthy debate continues in the academic world over definition and relevance of nationalism, interspersed sometimes with vicious interjections by the Left-Liberal apologists and closet communalists.

Ansari's Argument Does Not Apply to India

Former Vice President of India, Hamid Ansari, raked up this debate once. In a brief address during the so-called Congressional briefing hosted by the Indian American Muslim Council on the eve of India's Republic Day, Ansari made critical comments about governance and rule of law in India. 'In recent years, we have experienced the emergence of trends and practices that dispute the well-established principle of civic nationalism and interposes a new and imaginary practice of cultural nationalism,' he alleged. He accused the 'electoral majority' of presenting itself as a 'religious majority and monopolise political power'.

Ansari is a scholar and a former diplomat. He has every right to initiate a healthy debate over concepts like cultural and civic nationalism. But as someone trained in diplomatic nuances, he should have known the right time and forum to trigger such a debate.

Imprudence notwithstanding, Ansari was not alone in raking up the debate. In the West, the arrival of immigrants from West Asia and North Africa has triggered the debate on civic nationalism. The European liberals had initially welcomed these migrants with the slogan of 'multiculturalism'. But when the trickle became a flood leading to serious demographic and social challenges, including the resurgence of extreme Right-wing parties in several countries, majority of them abandoned that fad. Former German Chancellor Angela Merkel called even multiculturalism a 'sham'.

But some continue to argue that the immigrants should not be forced to adopt the culture of the host country while granting them equal citizenship as the natives, and that they should be allowed to follow their own culture, language, customs and practices. This multiculturalist argument came to be identified with the concept of civic or constitutional nationalism.

Ansari's comments should be seen in the background of this debate. The immigrant question, which is central to the civic nationalist argument, does not apply to India. The minorities in India—especially the Muslims and Christians—are not immigrants, but very much a part of this national society for millennia. They did not migrate. They only changed religion during the course of history. The cultural nationalists argue that mere change of religion does not uproot them from their cultural and civilizational identity.

Indian Nationalism Has Many Takers

A civic identity for minorities, distinct from their sociocultural identity, was a nineteenth century construction by the communalist leadership in India. The British had precipitated it through separate electorates on the basis of religion. Muhammad Ali Jinnah had immediately lapped up this so-called civic or constitutional arrangement as a compromise for Muslims to remain in India. That was the starting point of social disintegration in India, which finally culminated in Partition. Returning to civic nationalism discourse is tantamount to a rekindling of Jinnah's politics.

Indian nationalism was always viewed by its leaders as not merely a civic or constitutional agreement but a cultural-civilizational phenomenon. Not just leaders like Tilak, Gandhi, Savarkar and Aurobindo, even Jawaharlal Nehru, the demigod of liberalism, never disputed the 'cultural' aspect of Indian nationhood. In his famous 'Tryst with Destiny' address at midnight on 14 August 1947, Nehru exhorts that 'the soul of a nation, long suppressed, finds utterance'.

'At the dawn of history, India started on her unending quest, and trackless centuries are filled with her striving and the grandeur of her successes and, her failures. Through good and ill fortune alike she has never lost sight of that quest or forgotten the ideals which gave her strength,' he adds. What soul was he talking about? What nation? What ideals?

Delivering the annual convocation address at the Aligarh Muslim University in 1948, Nehru frankly questions the students:

> I have said that I am proud of our inheritance and our ancestors who gave an intellectual and cultural pre-eminence to India. How do you feel about this past? Do you feel that you are also sharers in it and inheritors of it and, therefore proud of something that belongs to you as much as to me? Or do you feel alien to it and pass it by without understanding it or feeling that strange thrill which comes from the realisation that we are the trustees and inheritors of this vast treasure?

Nehru said he was asking those questions because 'in recent years many forces have been at play diverting people's minds into wrong channels and trying to pervert the course of history'. Those forces appear to be active even now.

As regards to pluralism in India, the Constitution offers fullest religious freedom which was upheld by all the successive governments. Thomas Jefferson overthrew the Protestant constitutional and religious order in Massachusetts and Connecticut. Mormon religious practises like polygamy were banned by federal governments in America. The British parliament had designated Anglican bishops to the House of Lords. In India, such State intervention in religion, although desired in some cases, never happened.

The civic nationalists may understand that India's pluralism, too, is a product of its cultural nationalism.

Reprinted from THE PRINT, with permission of Printline Media Pvt. Ltd.

23

The Complex Roots of the Russia-Ukraine Conflict

It is a war between two Vladimirs. One, the indomitable President of Russia, Vladimir Putin, a strong and boisterous leader with decades of experience at strategy and statecraft; and another, the diminutive President of Ukraine, Volodymyr Zelenskyy, the Jewish-born actor-turned-politician with no experience of either. It is an uneven battle, between a Cold War giant with a strong military and a newly born nation state with an army less than half in size to its rival.

Putin insists that his actions were driven by security concerns that stem from the North Atlantic Treaty Organization's (NATO's) mischievous manoeuvres in Ukraine. But his refrain about 'denazification' of Ukraine indicates that it was not just about a military battle. The roots of this conflict lie in history and ideology. And that is where Vladimir, a ubiquitous first name in Russia, becomes relevant.

Vladimir the Great, the tenth-century grand prince of the millennia-old Kievan Rus empire, is considered the father of the modern Russian nation. But the problem is, Ukrainians think that, as the king of Kyiv in 980–1015 AD, he was the father of the Ukrainian nation too. Putin wants to determinedly contest it, not just academically, but physically. Vladimir the Great could not have been a father to many distinct nations, he insists.

'History will be kind to me, as I intend to write it,' Winston Churchill once remarked. Historic interpretations depend on who present them and with what force. In a long address to his countrymen, a few days before marching his tanks into Ukrainian territory, Putin dwelled at length on the history of Russia, forcefully demolishing the Ukrainian argument for a separate national identity. People of 'Rus', the empire built by Vladimir the Great, were all Russian, he concluded, insinuating that it was the Austro-Hungarians, Germans, Poles and Lithuanians, who, on different historic occasions, tried to manipulate the Ukrainians into believing that they were a separate people.

But the Ukrainians, too, have their history. The Ukrainians believe that theirs had been an independent nation for centuries with a distinct language and culture. Vladimir the Great's kingdom of Kyiv, the present-day capital of Ukraine, was an important and powerful empire during the second millennium and was never under the full control of the Russian Czars also, they argue.

It was only in 1922 that Ukraine became a part of the erstwhile Union of the Soviet Socialist Republics (USSR). Even then, Ukrainian Communists maintained a distinct identity from that of the Communist Party of the Soviet Union.

Putin was a trusted lieutenant of Boris Yeltsin during the latter's years in office as president of Russia after the USSR's collapse. In gratitude, Yeltsin chose Putin as his successor when he relinquished office in 1999. Putin is an avowed Russian nationalist, who continues to hold the view that the collapse of the Soviet Union was a 'catastrophe'. He believes, not wrongly, that Western powers were responsible for the travails of the great Russian nation, including the last time in 1991.

'Tame Russia' had been a project of many European

powers in the last millennium. It continued through the Cold War years. The famous Eisenhower Doctrine of 1957 was all about the containment of the Soviet Union. Stalin held deep suspicions about the West, so did his successors. After the collapse of the Soviet Union, Putin initially attempted to square up with the West by offering to join the European Union. But the doors were not opened for him. Not one to take humiliations lying down, Putin decided to teach the Europeans a lesson.

Besides history, there was, thus, an ideological angle too. The West treated the Russians as barbarians and their religion and politics as inferior. In retaliation, Putin did everything possible to undermine Western liberal political institutions by not only rejecting them, but also undermining them through digital interventions. His emphasis on ethno-cultural national identity squarely contradicts the West's modern geopolitical nation state. Ukraine's liberal democratic turn, for him, was thus tantamount to an ideological defeat of his brand of politics. Putin was unequivocal that 'true sovereignty of Ukraine is possible only in partnership with Russia'.

The Communists detested religion. At the Tehran Conference in 1943, when Churchill suggested that the support of the Pope be mobilized in order to contain Hitler, Stalin famously asked, 'How many divisions does the Pope have?' Putin is not anti-religion, but he does suspect that the Catholic powers were trying to weaken the Russian Orthodox identity by weaning away the Ukrainians. Incidentally, the Ukrainian President is a Jew, all the more a reason for Putin's suspicion.

It is this complex history and ideology behind the conflict that puts India in a difficult position. It could have not accepted Putin's basic proposition that Ukrainians were not a separate nation, without risking negating its stand on Tibet, Taiwan and other occupied or claimed countries by China. It also could not have wholly rejected the genuine security concerns of Russia in the face of the provocative actions by the NATO allies either.

Today, the global opinion is against Putin's actions. While India took a principled stand on opposing the war imposed on Ukraine, the optics of it standing with China at the United Nations are raising hackles in sections of the world. Can this great democratic nation continue to remain neutral for too long?

Reprinted from the HINDUSTAN TIMES, with permission of HT Media Ltd.

GOOD GOVERNANCE

'Empowering the individual means empowering the nation. And empowerment is best served through rapid economic growth with rapid social change.'[16]

—ATAL BIHARI VAJPAYEE
FORMER PRIME MINISTER OF INDIA

[16]'Good Governance Day 2020: Date, Significance and Quotes', *India Today*, 25 December 2020, http://tinyurl.com/m5ean62s. Accessed on 8 January 2024.

24

The 'Bhishma Pitamah' of Indian Politics

Atal Bihari Vajpayee—the very name invokes warm sentiments of goodwill across political and social spectrums. The world has seen many leaders. For some, leadership is a legacy handed down. They are born as leaders. Their greatness is drawn from their surnames. They are more like princelings than leaders. Some acquire greatness through their actions, their service and their projection. They remain leaders throughout their lifetime with the acquired greatness.

But there are some who command greatness by virtue of their very persona. Their very existence, even their memory, radiates greatness. Their aura remains even when they are not there. They don't just remain leaders, but become a phenomenon. Atal ji was one such rare phenomenon in Indian politics.

Rarely do we come across leaders who command respect across both sides of the political firmament. Rarer are leaders who had no adversaries. But in Atal ji, the country has seen a leader who can be described as '*Ajatshatru* (one without enemies)'.

Not without reason that Atal ji was also called the 'Bhishma Pitamah' of Indian politics. Bhishma, the legendary warrior of the epic Mahabharata, was known not only for his war-craft but also for his great wisdom. Bhishma epitomized Raj Dharma. He proffered it and practiced it too. In Atal ji, one saw the virtue of that Raj Dharma. Governance is not just a craft that one can skillfully manage. It is a dharma—a moral code. Bhishma was the first to articulate it proficiently.

Thomas Hobbes, a seventeenth century British philosopher and the father of the social contract theory, proposed that the state is a product of a contract between the rulers and the ruled. But in Indian philosophy, the state was seen as an instrument to uphold dharma. Out of Hobbes' social contract theory emerged the present-day democratic system, which believed that 'a society gets a government it deserves'.

But the Indian understanding of the statecraft was: '*Yatha Raja Tatha Praja* (As is the king, so are the subjects)'. Bhishma in Shanti Parva to Kautilya in Arthashastra, insisted that '*Raja Kalasya Karanam* (King is responsible for the times)'. In other words, it was believed that the rulers were responsible for molding the society. In that sense, good governance is not limited to delivering goods to the people; it is also about shaping the future of a nation.

In the West, right from the time of the Greeks, state and society were seen as separate, and often antagonistic entities. But Kautilya in Arthashastra erases that distinction and insists that a king is his kingdom only. It should not be understood as authoritarianism or dictatorship. Kautilya's insistence was that the king had no identity apart from his people. 'In the happiness of his people lies the happiness of the king,' exhorted Kautilya. That is the basis of Raj Dharma and Dharma Rajya.

Ancient Indian philosophers have talked about the concept of Yogakshema—well-behaving and well-being of the people. That too was stated as the basis of good governance or Raj Dharma.

The Shukla Yajurveda (6.31) includes a prayer wherein a king prays, 'let my subjects be satisfied, my herds be satisfied, my people be satisfied, let not my people be needy.' Happiness was not understood as mere material development, but the pervasive greater sense of unity, security and peace.

In Shanti Parva as also in Arthashastra, both Bhishma and Kautilya enumerate several qualities that are required for the ruler to uphold this Raj Dharma of bringing Yogakshema—all-round development of man and society. Kautilya's benchmarks for a true leader were daunting. He called for leaders who were Rajarshis. He says:

आत्मज्ञानं समारंभस्तितिक्षा धर्मनित्यता
यमर्थान्नापकर्षन्ति स वै राजर्शि: उच्यते।

(They who are not overwhelmed by the challenges of life owing to their knowledge, persistence, patience and virtue are the wise, deserving the position of leadership.)

निषेवते प्रशस्तानि निन्दितानि न सेवते
अनास्तिक: श्रद्धा एतद् राजर्शिन: लक्षणम्।

(The wise are those who adhere to their duties, who stand by their words, who praise the deserving, criticize the undeserving, who are untouched by selfish interest and who are revered for their virtues. Such people deserve the position of leadership.)

क्रोधो हर्षश्च दर्पश्च ह्रीस्तम्भो मान्यमानिता
यमर्थान्नापकर्षन्ति स वै राजर्शि: उच्यते।

(That person who overwhelms his anger, joy, sorrow and pride, who has no false modesty, neither confusion nor vanity, who can stay equanimous in mind at all times, is undoubtedly a wise deserving position for leadership.)

As we start judging leaders by those values, Atal ji stands out heads and shoulders above many others.

Atal Democracy

Jawaharlal Nehru passionately declared that India would be a democracy after Independence. But it was only Vajpayee who made it a true democracy by building the much-needed second national pole in the country's politics.

When Nehru announced that India shall adopt a democratic model of government, Gandhi wrote that he was not well-versed in those Western ideologies, but understood that democracy for independent India should be the Ram Rajya. 'By Ram Rajya, I do not mean a theocracy. It will be a state where the weakest shall have as much power as the strongest,' he wrote.

Deendayal Upadhyaya, the ideologue-leader of Bharatiya Jana Sangh, insisted that for a country like India, democracy should mean consensus building.

Atal ji sought to emulate these leaders in delivering his Raj Dharma. His positivity, transparency and openness to ideas had allowed him to understand and assimilate diverse strands of political opinion. 'Indian democracy's greatest strength is that we have always put the nation above politics,' Vajpayee once insisted.

Power was never a big attraction for him. People still remember his address in the parliament while relinquishing power in 1996 after 13 days of the government. 'Parties will come and go; governments will be made and unmade; but this nation should remain strong and its democracy should remain flourishing.' That was Vajpayee.

It was this detachment from power and dignified engagement with diverse shades of opinion that had helped him perform a herculean feat of forging a 23-party government and successfully running it for a full five years.

As Prime Minister (PM), Vajpayee delivered all-round

development in the country. Many people-centric initiatives took shape during his tenure as the PM. Those transformational initiatives include the Kisan Credit Card scheme, the Golden Quadrilateral, the Pradhan Mantri Gram Sadak Yojna, the National Rural Health Mission, the interlinking of rivers, the Sarva Shiksha Abhiyan, a separate ministry for tribal affairs, a revolutionary telecom policy and many more.

A shining example of his successful consensus building was the formation of three new states—Chhattisgarh, Jharkhand and Uttarakhand in 2000 in a peaceful manner.

Vajpayee Doctrine

India had 11 PMs before Vajpayee. However, only two were credited with having a doctrinal approach to governance. Nehru had Panchsheel as the sheet anchor of his foreign policy. Indira Gandhi too was credited with a doctrine that allowed interference in the neighbourhood for India's greater security. Apart from these two, the only other PM credited with a doctrinal approach to governance was Atal Bihari Vajpayee. Doctrines are the foundational principles that guide the policies of future governments.

The Vajpayee doctrine saw the nuclearization of India's security as an imperative. However, that doctrine also emphasized that those 'nuclear weapons were meant purely as a deterrent against nuclear adventure by an adversary'. 'No first use,' announced by Vajpayee in the wake of the nuclear tests in 1998 continues to guide India's nuclear policy.

On the neighbourhood too, Atal ji's views were doctrinal. 'We can change our friends but not neighbours,' he once told the Indian Parliament. That belief took him to Lahore by bus and allowed Pervez Musharraf a sojourn to Agra after his serious misadventures like the Kargil War and the Parliament attack. But Atal ji was also categorical that 'the overwhelming public sentiment in India was that no meaningful dialogue can be held with Pakistan until it abandons the use of terrorism as an instrument of its foreign policy'. Musharraf was sent back empty-handed.

In resolving the complex problem of Kashmir, the Vajpayee doctrine enunciated the principle of '*insaniyat, jamhuriyat and Kashmiriyat* (humanity, peace and the sanctity of Kashmiri people)'. In different forms and shades, that continues to guide Indian policy in the troubled region to this day.

Like any other public leader, Vajpayee too endured criticism. His doctrine was subjected to harsh scrutiny. But in the end, the Swayamsevak in him, which he always claimed himself to be, guided his actions, and the poet in him always rescued him.

Reprinted from CHINTAN–INDIA FOUNDATION BLOGS, *with permission of India Foundation.*

25

Achieving Growth with Balance

The world population crossed six billion in October 1999 and we added another two billion in two decades. On 15 November 2022 the world population crossed eight billion. Demographers at the UN predict that the planet will have 9.8 billion people in 2050 and 11.2 billion by 2100.[17]

India's population will cross 1.65 billion by 2050. China will see a decline in that year and its population will reduce to 1.3 billion. India will peak in that decade and thereafter, the numbers will start to recede and settle at 1.1 billion by 2100.[18]

For some demographers, population concerns are ill-founded. Rachel Snow of the United Nations Population Fund, for example, says that the world population growth is slowing down with more than 50 countries registering a population decline. Contrary to the UN's projection of 11.2 billion people on the planet by 2100, Snow insists that it will reduce to 8.5 billion by then. 'Eight billion people is potentially eight billion new ideas that will increase food production, very cool ways for people to learn on the

---

[17]'World Population Projected to Reach 9.8 Billion in 2050, and 11.2 Billion in 2100', *United Nations: Department of Economic and Social Affairs*, 21 June 2017, https://tinyurl.com/bdf8hfft. Accessed on 8 January 2024.

[18]'World Population Prospects 2022', *United Nations*, http://tinyurl.com/ykk4ftkc. Accessed on 29 January 2024.

internet… I am much more optimistic,' she says.[19]

Superabundance, a book published by Cato Institute in early 2022, argues that population growth was a good thing. 'On average, every additional human being created more value than he or she consumed. This relationship between population growth and abundance is deeply counterintuitive, yet it is true,' authors Marian Tupy and Gale Pooley argue.

Not all agree with the 'optimists'. Many rightly believe that more people means more mouths to feed, more exploitation of resources and more carbon emissions, which are detrimental to nature. Prime Minister (PM) Narendra Modi flagged this concern a few years ago. Cautioning that population explosion will cause many problems to future generations, he lauded those who stop 'to think before bringing a child to the world, whether they can do justice to the child, give them all that she or he wants'. Having smaller families is also a form of patriotism, he had said.

Most people tend to agree with PM Modi's observations. But demographics is a complex and often contentious subject. Incidentally, the developed West and China took a grim view of population growth in the last century and attempted population control. By the turn of this century, both countries witnessed low birth rates and consequently, a slowing down of population growth.

But at the same time, countries in the developing world, including in West Asia and Africa, continue to register higher population growth rates. It is projected that by 2100, close to 40 per cent of the world population will be residing in Africa.[20] That is, every second person in the world will

[19]UN Story, 'The World Population Has Reached 8 Billion – Now What? | Global Focus', *YouTube*, 12 November 2022, http://tinyurl.com/y55p9uuu. Accessed on 8 December 2024.

[20]'In 2100, 40% Of the World Population Will Be African', *WorldAtlas*,

be an African. Similarly, countries in the Muslim world are registering higher population growth rates—1.5 per cent, compared to the rest at 0.7 per cent. The Muslim population in the world is expected to reach 2.2 billion by 2030, according to the PEW Research Centre.[21] Egypt, the largest Arab country, had a population of 25 million in 1960, almost equal to that of South Korea. Six decades later, while South Korea's population doubled, Egypt's grew by more than four times to cross 110 million.

PEW Research Center's data projects the global Muslim population to be 2.8 billion (30 per cent of the world) by 2050 and the Christian population to be 2.9 billion (31 per cent). Hindus will constitute around 15 per cent of the world population by then.[22]

Data on religion needs to be carefully analyzed. Between 2010 and 2050, about 750 million Christians and 350 million Hindus will be added to the world population. But in the corresponding period, about 1.2 billion Muslims will join the global population. In the next four decades, the Christian share of the world population is projected to remain at 31.4 per cent while Hindus' share will decrease from 15 per cent to 14.9 per cent. But the share of the Muslim population will increase from 23.2 per cent to 29.7 per cent.[23]

India too cannot duck this trend. By 2050, India is expected to have over 1.3 billion Hindus, while the Muslim population

---

6 January 2020, http://tinyurl.com/zdwt26m4. Accessed on 8 January 2024.

[21]'The Future of the Global Muslim Population', *Pew Research Center*, 27 January 2011, http://tinyurl.com/bd83rxus. Accessed on 8 January 2024.

[22]'The Future of World Religions: Population Growth Projections, 2010–2050', *Pew Research Center*, 2 April 2015, http://tinyurl.com/bdcrjyse. Accessed on 9 January 2024.

[23]Ibid.

is likely to reach 311 million, making it the country with the largest Muslim population.[24]

It is here that the call given by the RSS (Rashtriya Swayamsevak Sangh) chief Mohan Bhagwat for a comprehensive population control policy, which should apply to all equally, and that no one should get any concessions, becomes relevant. Drawing attention to the challenges of unbalanced population growth, Bhagwat cited the creation of new countries like East Timor, South Sudan and Kosovo and said when there is a population imbalance, new countries are created. Countries are divided.[25]

There is a silver lining though. Globally, the population growth rates are declining and that includes Muslim populations as well. Although they continue to be high when compared to other communities, the fertility rates among Muslims too are falling. This trend was underscored by the National Family Health Survey in India. The total fertility rate (TFR)—the number of children each woman gives birth to—is a scientific way of projecting population growth. The TFR at around 2.2, with each family having a minimum of two children, is considered a balanced demographic growth. In 1951, the TFR among Muslims was over 5.4 and that among Hindus was over 3.2. According to recent data, the corresponding figures for Muslims and Hindus have dropped to 2.36 and 1.94 respectively.[26]

---

[24]Hackett, Conrad, 'By 2050, India to Have World's Largest Populations of Hindus and Muslims', *Pew Research Center*, 21 April 2015, https://tinyurl.com/4z6xnjjk. Accessed on 9 January 2024.

[25]Tiwary, Deeptiman, 'Population Imbalance Can Divide Countries, Need Policy for Population Control: Mohan Bhagwat', *The Indian Express*, 5 October 2022, https://tinyurl.com/2wteknk2. Accessed on 9 January 2024.

[26]'National Family Health Survey (NFHS-5) 2019-21', *mohfw.gov.in*, http://tinyurl.com/bdz7dv2z. Accessed on 29 January 2024.

French philosopher Auguste Comte's comment, 'demography is destiny', may not be completely true, yet different interested parties interpret it differently. A warped understanding of Comte leading to viewing women as reproductive machines must change.

The population will continue to grow, but it needs to be balanced growth. In our eagerness to make it 'destiny', we shouldn't make it into peril. We should be able to provide better living standards to the generations to come. We need five earths if everyone were to live like an American. As Gandhi said, nature can offer a free lunch, if only we control our appetite. The Indian answer will be sustainable consumption.

26

Decentralize and Empower States and Civil Society

For the country to tide over this emergency, greater empowered involvement of different stakeholders is imperative.

'Wait for Godot or wait for God?'—is a philosophical question that seekers direct at the masters. Godot was an enigmatic character created by the Irish playwright Samuel Beckett in his popular play, *Waiting for Godot.* In Beckett's play, two characters, Vladimir and Estragon, engage in animated discussions about various issues while waiting for the arrival of Godot, who never turns up. Waiting for Godot eventually became an allegory in the Christian tradition for man's urge for salvation which would never come.

Allegorically speaking, that appears to be the situation the second wave of the Covid-19 pandemic has pushed many in India towards. The healthcare establishment has been so overwhelmed that many patients find it difficult to access. Although called a wave, the second outburst of the pandemic turned out to be a tsunami.

We were able to handle the first wave efficiently. It was possible due to the timely steps taken by the government on one hand, and the disciplined response of the people on the other. But, over the last few months, complacency seems to have crept in. Going by the statements of the leaders in the government, they did not anticipate the virulence of the second wave. Citizens too seemed to be taking things lightly by not following pandemic protocols.

Social media is full of criticism these days. The larger share of the blame is laid at the doorstep of the government. It may partly be because people had high expectations from this government. They were convinced from last year's experience that the government knew how to handle the pandemic and would act swiftly. When things seem otherwise, they naturally blame the government.

Criticism is easy. But it must also be remembered that the challenge before the government is unprecedented. Nobody in the country has witnessed such a massive healthcare crisis in their lifetime. The last time that humanity experienced such a crisis was during the Spanish flu in 1918-19. An estimated 20 million Indians had perished during that pandemic.[27] Globally, over 100 million were said to have died of that virus.[28] The severity of the Spanish flu virus was such that Mahatma Gandhi, himself afflicted, had confided in a confidante that 'all interest in living has ceased'.

Covid-19 is not too dissimilar to the Spanish flu. Both spread through human contact, and nose and mouth were the infecting organs. There are lessons to be learnt from both the experiences.

One big lesson that the Covid-19 pandemic has taught is that a country of India's size and diversity needed greater decentralization. Decentralization does not simply mean the

---

[27]Kant, Lalit, and Randeep Guleria, 'Pandemic Flu, 1918: After Hundred Years, India Is as Vulnerable', *The Indian Journal of Medical Research*, Vol. 147, March 2018.

[28]Kettle, Martin, 'A Century On, Why Are We Forgetting the Deaths of 100 Million?', *The Guardian*, http://tinyurl.com/bdfntatu. Accessed on 9 January 2024.

Centre forwarding vaccines, medicines and oxygen supplies to the states for free distribution. It is about sufficiently empowering various stakeholders, including state governments, district and village administrations and non-governmental organizations (NGOs).

Right from the time of the making of the Indian constitution, there was a tendency to build a strong Centre. Many members of the Constituent Assembly had argued that we should make, not a federal, but a unitary constitution. Many expressed fears about Indian provinces developing secessionist tendencies if a federal system was put in place. The provincial representatives, on the other hand, were against centralization. B.R. Ambedkar, in his own wisdom, rightly impressed upon the members the need for having balanced decentralization of powers. He insisted that the dominance of the Centre will be 'expressly confined to emergencies only'.

There is a healthcare emergency today, no doubt. But it must be appreciated that greater empowered involvement of different stakeholders is imperative for the country to tide over this emergency. The differential and higher pricing of vaccines for states is unconvincing. Health being a state subject, the states are responsible for healthcare and need a greater independent role. Prime Minister Narendra Modi's principle of cooperative federalism should be at work.

Civil society and NGOs, which have been facing some difficulties in the recent past, need to be encouraged to supplement the government's efforts. In 1918, when British administrators had run away from the crisis and hidden in palatial rest houses in forests and remote areas, it was the media and civil society which had provided succour to the suffering millions. 'Never before, perhaps, in the history of India, have the educated and more fortunately placed members of the community, come forward in large numbers to help their poorer brethren in time of distress,' a British government report said.

Lastly, when a crisis befalls a nation, intellectual humility needs to be the way for all who matter. Just as success brings plaudits, crisis brings panning. There will be advice, both solicited and unsolicited, and criticism, both warranted and unwarranted. But in such a situation, the wise betray humility, not haughtiness. Haughtiness may win the day, but humility wins the race. It can be called the Socratic way.

When unreasonably condemned by the Athenian court for treason, Socrates, referring to an oracle's statement that he was the wisest among all citizens, humbly says: 'What's likely, gentlemen, is that in reality it's the god who is wise, and the oracle is saying, "he among you humans is wisest who, like Socrates, knows that he's really worth nothing when it comes to wisdom".'

Reprinted from HINDUSTAN TIMES, with permission of HT Media Ltd.

27

Why Public Morality and Unelected Institutions Integral to Democracy

India's democracy, as envisaged by the makers of its Constitution, thrived essentially because of the respect of the leaders for ethical constitutionalism and moral activism of the grassroots activists. Neither should see the other as an enemy and try to bring them down.

There was much scepticism about the idea of universal adult franchise during the making of the Indian Constitution.

The popular understanding of democracies is that they are elected governments. But democracies do not run merely on the basis of elected governments. In 2,500 years, democracies have developed systems of efficient checks and balances—elected and unelected institutions. Such a balance is critical to their success.

In recorded history, the Greeks were the first to experiment with models of government. There were monarchies, oligarchies and democracies among the Greek city-states of the fifth century BCE. Aristotle, the ancient Greek philosopher, wrote that while monarchies were for the benefit of the monarchs and oligarchies for the benefit of men with means, democracies were for the benefit of men without means. Plato, Aristotle's guru, was not fully in agreement. The city state of Sparta was an oligarchy while that of Athens was a raw democracy. Spartans ruled over Athens for a few decades. When they left, the Athenians held a court to punish the supporters of the Spartans. 21,000 Athenians, all men from privileged backgrounds, assembled in a stadium and voted to declare philosopher Socrates a collaborator with the Spartans. He was sentenced to death, prompting Plato to dismiss Athenian democracy as a 'kleptocracy'—a state of unrestrained political corruption.

Democracy has travelled a long way from those times. It has witnessed the rise of dictators like Hitler and Mussolini, but also many great democrats. Even today, Vladimir Putin in Russia and Joe Biden in America were elected through democratic elections very different from one another. The difference is that in the world's successful democracies like the US, UK and India, there is a fine balance between the elected and non-elected institutions with enough safeguards.

There was much scepticism about the idea of universal adult franchise during the making of the Indian Constitution. But Rajendra Prasad, the chairman of the Constituent Assembly, who became the first president of India, assured the Assembly's members about the raw political wisdom of the average Indian as also the strength of the other institutions to safeguard the democratic process. Seven decades of India's democratic experience bear testimony to the political maturity of the Indian people.

However, India has had its own bruises during this period. The infamous Emergency declared by Indira Gandhi taught an important lesson that Parliament, the elected branch of democracy often described as the 'temple of democracy', can become a circus and democracies can be imperilled if the rulers succeed in jeopardizing the other pillars like the judiciary and free press.

Mahatma Gandhi was not a big admirer of the parliamentary system. He never uttered a harsh word against anybody but used words such as 'sterile woman' and 'prostitute' for the British parliamentary system. Gandhi's view was that in the British system, the parliament works only for partisan interest—and not for the national interest. He wrote in *Harijan* in January 1937:

> By political independence I do not mean an imitation to the British House of Commons, or the Soviet rule of Russia or the Fascist rule of Italy or the Nazi rule of Germany. They have systems suited to their genius. We must have ours suited to ours... I have described it as Ram Rajya—sovereignty of the people based on pure moral authority.

B.R. Ambedkar too described democracy in India as 'only a top-dressing' on Indian soil 'which is essentially undemocratic'. In his famous 'Three Warnings' speech, Ambedkar warned that only constitutional means and institutions should be used hereafter instead of the means used during the freedom movement. He also underscored the importance of social democracy for the success of political democracy. Both were responding to the experiences of their times—Gandhi was referring to the tyranny of the British rule and Ambedkar was responding to the oppressive caste system. Neither was against democracy, but both were against the idea of 'majoritarian rule'. For Gandhi, democracy meant the weak getting the same chance as the strong. For Ambedkar, it was about giving voice to the voiceless.

For democracies to succeed, both Gandhi and Ambedkar believed that the parliamentary majorities need to be restrained through constitutional ethics and public morality. Constitutional ethics are about leaders respecting constitutional order, conventions and institutions. The Americans have a written constitution, the British don't. Yet, both developed healthy conventions that safeguard their democracies. There is a beautiful convention in America of the outgoing president leaving a hand-written letter for the incoming one, which the new incumbent of the White House would get to see on the first day in office. 'We are just temporary occupants of this office. That makes us guardians of those democratic institutions and traditions — like rule of law, separation of powers, equal protection and civil liberties… Regardless of the push and pull of daily politics, it's up to us to leave those instruments of our democracy at least as strong as we found them,' Barack Obama wrote in his letter to Donald Trump in January 2017. The elected must protect all the unelected instruments of democracy—judiciary, media and civic organizations.

Gandhi's greater emphasis was on public morality. He insisted that for India's democracy to succeed, the Congress should convert itself into a *lok sevak sangh* and work at the grassroots for the social, economic and moral independence of the people. True Gandhians chose syndication at the grassroots rather than election to Parliament or legislative assemblies.

India's democracy, as envisaged by the makers of its Constitution, thrived essentially because of the respect of the leaders for ethical constitutionalism and moral activism of the grassroots activists. Neither should see the other as an enemy and try to bring them down.

28

Ram Rajya: A Moral Sovereignty

Both Mahatma Gandhi and B.R. Ambedkar were looking at the concept of Ram Rajya from their respective prisms—Gandhi from a more pragmatic prism and Ambedkar from a literal one. But both highlight the fact that a just system should be one where the weak are protected and their voices heard.

'Hinduism is a movement, not a position; a process, not a result; a growing tradition, not a fixed revelation,' wrote eminent scholar, politician and statesman Dr Sarvepalli Radhakrishnan in his seminal work *The Hindu View of Life*. He further says:

> Precious as are the echoes of God's voice in the souls of men of long ago, our regard for them must be tempered by the recognition of the truth that God has never finished the revelation of His wisdom and love. Besides, our interpretation of religious experience must be in conformity with the findings of science. As knowledge grows, our theology develops. Only those parts of the tradition which are logically coherent are to be accepted as superior to the evidence of the senses and not the whole tradition.

Unlike the Semitic religions, Hinduism is not a religion of 'believers'. 'Unless you believe, you will not understand,' St Augustine of Hippo had exhorted early Christians of the

Roman empire. But Hinduism allowed inquiry and wanted men to be seekers, rather than mere believers. Ram and the Ramayana are divine for many. Gandhi called Ram his personal deity. But Ambedkar did not agree much with Ram. He even challenged the Ramayana, going to the original by Valmiki, in his *Riddles in Hinduism*. However, there is a common aspect in Gandhi and Ambedkar's stances—both argued from a logical perspective, not from blind faith or blind hatred.

Whether Ram was a historical person or not did not bother Gandhi much. What mattered to him was the concept of 'Ram Rajya'. In his view, Ram Rajya essentially meant equal rights to 'prince and pauper'. Even during his two visits to Ayodhya, the abode of his deity Ram, in 1921 and 1929, Gandhi's rhetoric was about standing up for the weak and the meek. Addressing the saints of Ayodhya on the banks of the Sarayu River during his visit in February 1921, he resorted to his favourite subject of Ram Rajya. He chose cow protection as the point of reference to tell saints, 'Praying to God for our own protection is a sin as long as we do not protect the weak...We need to learn to love the way Ram loved Sita.' There is no way to achieve Ram Rajya or *swaraj* without observing this *svadharma*, he told them.

Meanwhile, Ambedkar's criticism of the Ramayana was based on his perception of certain events. He believed, not necessarily correctly, that Ram upheld the Varnashrama system and had killed a Dalit saint called Shambuka. Ambedkar writes:

> Some people seem to blame Ram because he...without reason killed Shambuka. But to blame Ram for killing Shambuka is to misunderstand the whole situation. Ram Raj was...based on Chaturvarnya. As a king, Ram was bound to maintain Chaturvarnya. It was his duty therefore to kill Shambuka, the Shudra, who had transgressed his

class and wanted to be a Brahmin. This is the reason why Rama killed Shambuka.

Many scholars insist that the story of Shambuka's killing was an interpolation. Ambedkar was also critical, probably on more valid grounds, of Ram's treatment of Sita. He saw Ram Rajya as unjust and patriarchal and commented on Ram's dismissal of Sita to forests the second time as 'there are not wanting Hindus who use this as grounds to prove that Ram was a democratic king when others could equally well say that he was a weak and cowardly monarch.'

Both Gandhi and Ambedkar were looking at the concept of Ram Rajya from their respective prisms—Gandhi from a more pragmatic prism and Ambedkar from a literal one. But both highlight the fact that a just system should be one where the weak are protected and their voices heard. The search for such a just and equitable system where there is harmony between the ruler and the ruled has been carried on by political pundits for millennia. Socrates, the ancient Greek philosopher, was asked to consume poison by the democratic assembly of 21,000 citizens of Athens. His sin was that he supported the oligarchy of the 30 ruling tyrants of Sparta, a neighbouring city state. Socrates believed that the rule by a select class of wise men, like the oligarchy in Sparta, is better than a democracy based on mass hysteria as that in Athens. Tyrants in ancient Greek regimes were those who usurped the role of the monarch; not necessarily the way we understand its meaning today. Plato and Aristotle detested both systems—the cruel authoritarianism of Sparta and the mobocracy of Athens.

Plato's panacea was 'philosopher kings'. As Bhishma tells Yudhishthira in the 'Shanti Parva' of the Mahabharata, which was repeated by Chanakya in Arthashastra:

प्रजासुखे सुखं राज्ञः प्रजानां तु हिते हितम्।
नात्मप्रियं हितं राज्ञः प्रजानां तु प्रियं हितम्।।

(The happiness of the ruler lies in the happiness of his subjects. It is not what the ruler likes that matters, but only what people like.)

In the 'Yuddha Kanda' of the Ramayana, sage Valmiki narrates certain characteristics of Ram Rajya or Ram's kingdom:

- While Rama was ruling the kingdom, there were no widows to lament, nor was there any danger from wild animals, nor any fear of diseases. Every creature felt pleased.
- Everyone was intent on virtue. Turning their eyes towards Ram alone, creatures did not kill one another.
- While Ram was ruling the kingdom, people survived for thousands of years, with thousands of their progeny, all free from illness and grief.
- Trees there bore flowers and fruits regularly, without any injury by pests and insects. Clouds were raining on time and the wind was delightful to the touch.
- All the people were endowed with excellent characteristics. All were engaged in virtue.

Ram Rajya is envisioned as a state of governance where the ruler is wise enough to place the good of the people above the interest of his own. But then, who will determine what is good and bad? Nietzsche, the German philosopher, had interpreted 'good' as 'whatever augments the feeling of power, the will to power, power itself, in man', inadvertently becoming the darling of Hitler and the Nazis. Plato's 'philosopher kings' also became authoritarian when the Romans invested divinity in them and philosophers like Nietzsche gave weird interpretations of power. Julius Caesar commissioned dozens of sculptors to make different sculptures of him, while Hitler revelled in his wisdom of a 'superior race'. Such smugness and self-righteousness have produced cruel authoritarians throughout history.

Ram presented a different ideal. Valmiki used two phrases with profound meaning to describe Ram, whom he called 'विग्रहवान धर्मः (the epitome of morality)'. Those phrases are: Ram 'अराधनाय लोकस्य (worshipped people)' and 'राज्यम उपासित्वा (worshipped the kingdom)'. He did not believe in his infallibility nor was he overpowered by any superiority complex. When his mother, Kausalya, asked him after his return to Ayodhya whether he had killed Ravan, Ram's reply was: 'Mahagyani, Mahapratapi, Mahabalshali, Akhand Pandit, Mahan Shivbhakt, author of Shiv Tandav Stotra, the mighty Lankesh was killed by his own ego'.

That is why Gandhi summed up Ram Rajya as 'the sovereignty of the people based on pure moral authority'.

Reprinted from THE DAILY GUARDIAN.

HOME AND THE WORLD

'India of the ages is not dead nor has she spoken her last creative word; she lives and has still something to do for herself and the human peoples.'[29]

—SRI AUROBINDO

[29]Sri Aurobindo, *The Renaissance in India and Other Essays on Indian Culture*, Sri Aurobindo Ashram Publication Department, Pondicherry, 1997.

29

Beijing Wants 'Business as Usual': But Delhi Is Having None of It

Adam Smith's book, *The Wealth of Nations*, is well-known. His other book, *The Theory of Moral Sentiments*, though equally influential, is lesser-known. Smith raises a hypothetical scenario of ethical conflict in it, asking what would a European do if the great Chinese empire were to be swallowed up by an earthquake. He would obviously express sorrow, make 'melancholy reflections' upon the precariousness of human life, and might also speculate on how this disaster would impact commerce in Europe. 'And when all this fine philosophy was over, he would pursue his business or his pleasure, with the same ease and tranquillity, as if no such accident had happened,' Smith concludes.

Wang Yi, the Chinese foreign minister, wanted to do something similar during his visit to India in 2022. After all the disasters in bilateral relations, he quietly walked into Delhi to tell the Indian leadership that the two should get along with 'business as usual'. Wang was at his pontificating best as if nothing serious had happened between the two countries. 'As mature and rational major developing countries, China and India should not let the border issue define or affect the overall development of the bilateral relationship,' he told his counterpart, S. Jaishankar. He talked about a three-point approach: viewing bilateral relations with a long-term vision, developing a win-win mentality about each other's development and cooperating in multilateral processes. India responded with its three points: mutual respect, mutual sensitivity and mutual interest.

This style is typical of China and has been played out several times in the past. The Border Peace and Tranquility Agreement of 1993 was also a product of this Chinese trickery. After making incursions into Indian territory in the winter of 1986 at Sumdorong Chu Valley in Arunachal Pradesh, they dug in their heels for seven years before forcing a treaty that provided a principle of peace and tranquillity but didn't protect India's sovereign interests. Even that principle has been violated several times subsequently in the last three decades.

The Chinese follow the formula—'what I occupy is mine, what I claim is to be debated'. Wang Yi's proposal about a 'long-term vision' amounted to India accepting the present standoff as normalcy. Fortunately, the Indian leadership refused to buy this 'new normal', with Jaishankar insisting on peace and tranquillity along the Line of Actual Control as a precondition for normalcy.

The Narendra Modi government has affected an important shift in India's border policy with China that includes, besides proactive diplomacy, strong ground posturing as well. While continuing with the military-led talks over disengagement, India, during the two-year standoff, also participated in at least eight rounds of the Working Mechanism for Consultation and Coordination, a process to address the outstanding border issues. But, it simultaneously kept up ground offensive by deploying men and weapons in large numbers. If the Chinese moved their field guns and military aircraft, India too did the same.

Despite Doklam and Ladakh, the Chinese don't seem to realize that the current regime in India thinks differently and has a different approach. They continue with the old practice of upping the ante before every important bilateral visit to upset the Indian agenda by introducing new issues. Wang Yi's visit to Pakistan before coming to Delhi was one such old trick, which they play every time a senior Chinese leader visits India. Wang attended Pakistan's military parade where the Chinese-made J-10C fighter jets were flown for the first time. China supplied a full squadron of 25 jets to Pakistan recently.

In a deliberate provocation to India, Wang chose the Organisation of Islamic Conference Council of Foreign Ministers, held in Islamabad on 22 March to make unwarranted reference to Kashmir in a clear violation of the restraint hitherto followed by both countries in each other's internal matters. India never publicly articulated its views on Xinjiang or Tibet despite justifiable reasons. Naturally, the Indian side has forcefully conveyed its disapproval of his Kashmir references, both through an immediate media response naming Wang Yi in person and also at the discussion table in Delhi forcing Wang on the defensive.

On the issue of relations with China, there are hawks and hyper-realists in India. But the current regime has always taken a realistic and pragmatic approach in dealing with its important and troublesome neighbour. Both the External Affairs Minister and the National Security Advisor of India have been able to convey Delhi's position firmly but politely to Wang, sending him back almost empty-handed.

Wang Yi's reference to cooperation at the multilateral level also included co-opting India on the Ukraine issue. After India abstained from the vote on Ukraine at the United Nations Security Council (UNSC) and the UN, both the Russians and the Chinese have tried to project it as India's support to them. The Russian envoy at the UN, Dmitry Polyanski, publicly thanked India clubbing it with China, Kenya and Gabon, 'who were brave to withstand US hand-twisting before the vote'. The Chinese media went overboard suggesting it as India's change of heart.

India's stand on Ukraine is markedly different from that of China. China justifies Russia's aggression in Ukraine in the name of security concerns. However, India takes a different view. India is committed to international rule of law and respect for the territorial integrity and sovereignty of nations. It stood for a diplomatic resolution of disputes and opposed war. At the time of its abstention at the UN, India made its stand clear by asking for a cessation of conflict, immediate de-escalation of tensions and quiet and constructive diplomacy.

When the Nazi general Himmler battered Warsaw in Poland in 1944, turning 80 per cent of the city into rubble, Hitler shed crocodile tears, blaming the Russians, French and British for the plight of the Poles. Putin is doing the same by pounding Ukrainian cities, blaming the West and NATO. Notwithstanding several justifications from both sides, it's a war for supremacy over Eurasia, and China sees benefits in this new Cold War.

For India, it is as much about principles as about interests.

30

Democracy in South Asia

Interestingly, two leaders have a serious problem with the Rashtriya Swayamsevak Sangh (RSS) at the same time. One is Imran Khan, the former Prime Minister (PM) of Pakistan. Khan complained that he was unable to build strong ties with India because of the 'RSS ideology and what happened in Kashmir'. At the Central-South Asia conference held at Tashkent, Khan made similar comments, insisting that 'the ideology of RSS' had come in the way of resumption of dialogue between the two countries.

Another leader who finds a similar problem with the RSS is the senior Congress leader in India, Rahul Gandhi. '...we have to protect our institutions. But all the institutions are in the hands of RSS,' he bemoaned once. He has also called upon the Opposition parties that are against the RSS and PM Narendra Modi to come together.

It could be a strange coincidence that the two leaders on the losing side of the spectrum in two neighbouring countries find fault not with their own politics but the RSS for their ill-fortunes at the same time. What both of them should realize is that it is the democratic systems in the two countries that are coming in the way of their fortunes, not the RSS.

The RSS is an integral and influential part of India's democratic system. After India became independent, the RSS submitted a written constitution for itself in 1949, even before the country got one for its people. When the Indian democracy was usurped by Indira Gandhi in 1975–77 through the infamous Emergency, it was the RSS that stood up as a bulwark against Indira's dictatorship and worked for restoring democracy.

The Economist wrote on 12 December 1976:

> The underground campaign against Mrs Gandhi claims to be the only non-left wing revolutionary force in the world, disavowing both bloodshed and class struggle. The ground troops of this operation (the underground movement), consist of tens of thousands of cadres who are organised to the village level into four men cells. Most of them are RSS regulars, though more and more new young recruits are coming in. The other underground parties which started out as partners in the underground have effectively abandoned the field to the Jana Sangh and RSS.[30]

Rahul's claim that he was not interested in power reminds one of the 'sour grapes' analogy. Power, in any case, is nowhere in sight in near future for him and his party, which is shrinking by every passing election. It is the maturity of Indian democracy that rejects politics of dynasty and entitlement that Rahul proudly flaunted in that function claiming he was born 'in centre of power'. In a difficult South Asian neighbourhood, Indian democracy stands out as a beacon of hope and confidence.

One important factor that helped countries in the subcontinent stabilize as democracies is India's shining example. In their hour of crisis, both Sri Lanka and Pakistan look up to

[30]'The Opposition To Indira Wins Friends And Influence', *Hindu Vivek Kendra*, http://tinyurl.com/y832jfv7. Accessed on 12 January 2024.

Indian democracy. Leaders on both sides of the establishment in these countries are seen today singing paeans of India's democratic virtue and seeking its support.

It is India's example that has motivated other neighbours like Nepal and Bhutan to turn to democracy. After a short-lived stint in 1959, Nepal turned firmly to democracy in the 1990s leaving the monarchic past behind. In Bhutan, the monarchy itself facilitated the establishment of democracy in 2008. The Maldives has also consistently laboured to build a democratic polity since the 1968 referendum. Bangladesh struggled initially with democracy, with military rulers repeatedly interrupting its smooth progress, finally settling down as a functioning democracy from the 1990s.

This democratization process in South Asia is significant because the other major player in the region, China, which has close ties with many countries in the region, has an entirely different political system. The Chinese aid that flows into the region also comes with its unwholesome political influence.

Sadly, the Western commentators fail to appreciate this regional reality and try to subject countries to undue pressure in the name of democratic deficit. A case in point is the Summit for Democracy, hosted by the US Department of State in 2021. In our neighbourhood, while Nepal and Maldives received an invitation, Bhutan and Sri Lanka were denied the same. While a wobbling democracy like Pakistan was qualified in the eyes of the US State Department for the Summit, a more functional one in Bangladesh was not. Prime Minister of India, Narendra Modi, addressed that Summit virtually. China, expectedly, not only opposed that Summit, but also released a report on the 'status of US democracy', calling it 'dysfunctional'.

India believes in non-interference in the affairs of other nations. Yet, its benign influence as the world's largest functional democracy should help its neighbours in finding answers to their present challenges, lest they fall victims to authoritarianism and autocratic regimes once again.

Reprinted from CHINTAN–INDIA FOUNDATION BLOGS, *with permission of India Foundation.*

31

Bangladesh Must Keep Up Sheikh's Secular Legacy

A.K. Abdul Momen, Bangladesh's foreign minister, had tried to downplay the communal violence that rocked the country in 2021, blaming 'enthusiastic media and individuals' for spreading 'cooked up stories' to embarrass the government. He denied that there were any rapes or destruction of temples and insisted that the government is 'committed to religious harmony'.

It is true that more than 500 people have been arrested by the police and action has been initiated against them. The government is also compensating the victims. There is also no denying the fact that the condition of minorities like Hindus, Buddhists and Christians has been better under the Sheikh Hasina regime. Representation of Hindus has steadily improved in Bangladesh's Jatiya Sangsad in the last three elections. There are 18 elected Hindu MPs (Members of Parliament) today, 17 of whom are from the ruling Awami League.[31] Their representation in government services has also increased in the last decade. Minorities constitute about seven per cent in civic employment and 10 per cent in police jobs. Several

[31]'Seventeen Hindu Members Have Been Elected in 11th Parliament in Bangladesh', *Struggle for Hindu Existence*, http://tinyurl.com/2wvvm4ce. Accessed on 29 January 2024.

Hindus occupy senior positions. Justice Surendra Kumar Sinha became the Chief Justice of Bangladesh Supreme Court in 2015. He had to resign after three years because of political, not communal, reasons.

Durga Puja *mandap*s get financial support from the government besides security for major ones. Sheikh Hasina gave the slogan, '*Dhormo jar jar, utsob shobar* (Religion as per one's own, but festivals common to all)'. As a result, the number of Puja mandaps went up. There were over 30,000 Durga Pujas in 2017 and 31,272 in 2018.[32] Even after the Covid-19 pandemic, the numbers were around the same. Sheikh Hasina also took special care to support Dhaka's Dhakeshwari Temple, when the management was facing challenges.

But there is another side too. Governments in South Asia tend to downplay communal cleavages and their violent fallout. Bangladesh is no exception. There is ample visual evidence about the extent of arson and violence during the Durga Puja. That the violence was spread over more than 70 districts proves that it was a well-planned attack. Besides the Bangladesh Nationalist Party (BNP) and Jamaat cadres, there were many among the perpetrators owing their allegiance to the ruling party too.

Hasina came down heavily on the radical Islamists responsible for atrocities during the formation years of Bangladesh. War crime tribunals have ordered the execution of many Islamists responsible for brutalities during the liberation war, including senior leaders of Jamaat-e-Islami and Salauddin Quader Chowdhury of the BNP. Hasina demonstrated her resolve against Islamic terror by quickly punishing the

---

[32]Chaudhury, Dipanjan Roy, 'Sheikh Hasina Gifts 1.5 Bigha Land to Biggest Hindu Temple in Bangladesh', *The Economic Times*, 18 October 2018, http://tinyurl.com/mr235uf7. Accessed on 12 January 2024.

perpetrators of the July 2016 bombings at the Holey Artisan cafe, in which 22 people were massacred.[33] Seven Islamists have been given death sentences in that terror attack. But when it comes to atrocities against the minorities, the Hasina government fails to show similar determination, baffling many secular-minded eminences and emboldening radicals. A report by human rights organization, *Odhikar*, states that between 2007 and 2019, 12 people belonging to other religions were killed, 1,536 injured and 1,013 properties and 390 temples attacked. Hindus bore the brunt of this bigotry. The human rights organization, Ain o Salish Kendra (ASK), reported 3,710 attacks exclusively on Hindu communities (10 deaths and 862 injuries) between January 2013 and September 2021.

Islamist radicalism is on the rise in Bangladesh despite efforts by the Hasina government. Madrasas are booming. As per the government's estimates, the number of Qawmi madrasas could be anything between 13,902 and 33,000. There are another 70,000 mosque-based Furqania maktabs and more than 4,000 Hafizia madrasas, as of 2008, which were not included in the above numbers.

There were reports about tinkering with the country's 'secular' education curriculum. In 2017, poems and stories by Sunil Gangopadhyay, Sarat Chandra Chattopadhyay, Humayun Azad and Rabindranath Tagore were quietly removed from school textbooks and replaced with more 'Islamist' pieces.

Bangladesh's current challenge is not just about security for its minorities. It is about its larger identity. There was a time when the phrase 'Bengali Muslim' used to be considered an oxymoron. But thanks to the efforts of leaders like Fazlul Huq

---

[33]'Holey Artisan Cafe: Bangladesh Islamists Sentenced to Death for 2016 Attack', *BBC News*, 27 November 2019, http://tinyurl.com/2mk4387p. Accessed on 9 January 2024.

during and after Partition, and Mujibur Rahman during and after the liberation war, such an identity has been created—it was to be secular, socialist, nationalist and democratic. Fazlul Huq had refused to toe the Muslim League line in Bengal. He started the Krishak Praja Party, defeated the League's Islamist strongman Khawaja Nazimuddin in 1937, opposed the Partition and, together with leaders of the Congress like Sarat Chandra Bose, wanted Bengal to become an independent country.

'Bangabandhu' Sheikh Mujibur Rahman, the founder of the Awami League, had infused secularism as a founding principle of the constitution in 1972. Sheikh Hasina is carrying that legacy of a Bengali Muslim, which is being consistently eroded.

General Ziaur Rahman and his successor General Ershad were primarily responsible for negating Bangabandhu's vision. Ziaur got the constitution amended in 1979 to remove the word 'secularism'. Ershad declared Islam as the 'state religion' in 1988. Although Hasina restored 'secularism' in the constitution through the Fifteenth Amendment in 2011, the country continues to maintain the odd distinction of being a secular country and an Islamic state simultaneously.

Hasina's challenge, before she passes the baton on to her successor, will be to restore the dream and legacy of her father. Incidentally, it is a challenge for all of South Asia, since we are one people and communalism in one place has the potential to foment the same in another.

32

India and China: The Road Ahead

India and China are two big neighbours. Both are fast developing nations with global ambitions. The challenge lies in managing this competition in a healthy manner and not allowing it to lead to confrontation.

Nations are products of their histories. China had a 'century of humiliation' from which it came out in the middle of the last century to build a modern socialist state. A long war and a long march led by Mao Zedong preceded its liberation.

India too faced centuries of colonial occupation before it finally unshackled itself around the same time as China. India achieved it through Mahatma Gandhi's non-violent resistance movement.

Historical and civilizational experiences of the two countries shaped future growth trajectories of both. Right at the onset of India's Independence, Prime Minister (PM) Jawaharlal Nehru laid down certain benchmarks for India's foreign policy.

India will build an Asian alliance. Nehru hosted the first Asian Relations Conference in March 1947, even before India became fully independent. Almost all the important Asian leaders were present at that conference.

India will remain non-aligned; it will also retain its sovereign autonomy. Nehru was one of the tall leaders of the Non-Aligned Movement (NAM) together with Abdel Nasser of Egypt, Josip Broz Tito of the erstwhile Yugoslavia and Sukarno of Indonesia.

India will strive for peace and non-aggression; but

will continue to build strength for its self-defence. Nehru championed Panchsheel—the five principles of peaceful coexistence, but also initiated India's nuclear programme during his prime ministership.

India continued its journey on these principles. There were no major U-turns in its foreign policy in the last seven decades. It largely remained a continuum.

Nehru, unfortunately, became obsessed about ideas like Panchsheel, and faltered in the process. Leaders like P.V. Narasimha Rao, Atal Bihari Vajpayee and Narendra Modi added the important dimension of pragmatism during their tenures. Prime Minister Modi aggressively pursued the policies of neighbourhood first, sovereign autonomy and de-hyphenation in relations with countries. Diaspora diplomacy is his unique contribution to foreign policy.

China, under Mao, developed its foreign policy based on its own historical experience. The violent Long March of the Chinese Red Army continued after the creation of the Communist China in 1949. Annexation of Tibet on the one hand and the involvement in the Korean War on the other, had shaped its foreign policy in the initial years into a machismo one.

It didn't take long for India to experience it. Nehru's 'peaceful coexistence' came face to face with Mao's 'armed coexistence' in just a decade's time when the People's Liberation Army (PLA), after completing its occupational mission in Tibet, stood at its doorstep in early 1960s. A war and a period of chill in diplomatic relations ensued.

Efforts began in the 1980s to find a common purpose once again in the bilateral relationship.

Deng Xiaoping, the supreme leader, told the visiting Indian PM Rajiv Gandhi in 1988 that the two countries should strive together to make the impending twenty-first century as the 'Asian Century'.

India supported China's entry into the World Trade Organization towards the end of the last century.

Wen Jiabao, the Chinese premier, on a visit to India in 2010, even reminded New Delhi that the history of tensions between the two countries was just five decades old while the history of friendship and bonhomie was over 2,000 years. 'China and India are connected by mountains and rivers and enjoy a traditional friendship dating back more than 2,000 years', he said. Yet, here we are today, standing eyeball to eyeball once again. It is instructive to analyse the history and strategize about the best course for future.

1. Peaceful Rise: India has a proclaimed 'ambition to rise as an influential and responsible global power'. But its rise has been and will continue to be peaceful and beneficial to other countries. China has grown impressively in the last few decades. It continues to grow and aspires to become the world's largest economy in a couple of decades. Can the current Chinese leadership ensure that it will be a 'peaceful rise'?

Deng, as the supreme leader, recognized this imperative and managed the rise of Chinese in a very innocuous manner in the 1980s and 1990s. His famous dictum—'Hide your strength—Bide your time'—ensured that China's rise didn't rattle other countries.

The foundations for China's unprecedented growth were laid during Deng's regime in a very silent and unobtrusive manner. But President Xi Jinping displayed a different style. Deng's reticence has been replaced by Xi's aggression and haughtiness. Phrases like 'Wolf Warrior Diplomacy' and 'Big Power Diplomacy' became ubiquitous under Xi's rule after 2013. It is for the Chinese leadership to think if this approach is really helping the country.

2. Talking and Engagement: When the rise of nations is not that peaceful, the next important imperative is to be engaged in talking. Mature leaders of India and China are talking with each other regularly. Prime Minister Modi and President Xi have met 17 times so far. They developed a good mutual friendship also.

At the height of the Cuban missile crisis in 1962, the Soviets and the Americans were almost on the brink of a nuclear war until President John F. Kennedy of America decided one afternoon to reach out to the Soviet President Nikita Khrushchev with the help of his brother Robert Kennedy and the Soviet Ambassador to Washington, Anatoly Dobrynin. That one message had saved the Soviet Union and America from a disastrous war and the world from the Armageddon.

The Chinese friends these days suggest that the border dispute should be decoupled from bilateral trade and civilian relations. On the surface, it sounds very benign. However, its implications need to be analysed carefully. In fact, it is not a new suggestion either. When PM Rajiv Gandhi visited China in 1988, the intrinsic understanding was that the border dispute may be frozen for some time and other issues may be taken up for bilateral discussion.

Freezing borders means freezing on both sides. But if one side continues to violate the borders, the other side cannot be expected to 'decouple' or 'freeze' it. Just as talks and terror cannot go together, talks and border violations also do not go together.

Hence, India and China should actively talk about the border dispute rather than trying to put it on the backburner. The very first principle of the India-China border negotiations was that neither country would alter the status quo, nor any armed conflict would be allowed. Both the points have been violated by China during the recent stand-off. Hence, to start with, China should restore status quo ante in the western sector to April this year.

3. Trust Deficit and Perception Management: Both India and China are populous nations. People in both the countries are highly nationalistic. Managing perception about each other among the general populace is an important challenge for leaders of both countries. It is important to ensure that people of the other country do not look at us as enemies. In the era of the extensive reach of social media, this perception management becomes even more important.

The 'trust deficit' that is often talked about is not limited to leaders alone. It is among the people too. China needs to work hard on this front. Recent survey by the Washington-based Pew Research Center highlighted growing negative perception about China in many important countries. Once important trade partners of China, countries like Canada and Australia also, today, witness steep rise of anti-China sentiments among their citizens.

India is no exception. Anti-China sentiment among the ordinary people of India is at its all-time high today. There are voluntary campaigns to boycott Chinese goods and products. Some Chinese scholars sneer at it. As a democracy, India cannot afford to ignore the popular sentiment altogether, nor can it trample upon it.

There is a famous saying that 'we cannot choose our parents'. We cannot choose our neighbours either. We have to learn to live together. India and China have no option but to live and grow together. 'Growing together' requires a mindset different from that of mere 'growing'.

We hear a lot about 'big power diplomacy' in China these days. Big power diplomacy is not about the size of the country or population or military strength. It is about the mindset. What the world experiences is big brother diplomacy. The need of the hour is 'big heart diplomacy'.

Reprinted from SWARAJYA, with permission of Kovai Media Pvt. Ltd.

33

A World Union Based on Resurgent Asianism

Hindu and Buddhist priests and monks were the first people to carry India's influence across its boundaries two millennia ago. The Buddhist monks largely chose the land routes with the exception of Sri Lanka, where Buddhism was taken by the son and daughter of emperor Ashoka—Mahinda and Sanghamitra—in third century BCE. Monks from Northern India had travelled to Tibet, China, Mongolia and Bhutan carrying the religion of Buddha. On the other hand, the Hindu priests too managed to reach countries as far as Cambodia, Vietnam and Indonesia in the initial centuries of the first millennium carrying with them the benign religion of Hinduism. While there were references to instances of the Greek and Hindu scholars exchanging philosophical ideas in the pre-Christian era, recorded evidence of Hindu influence over the countries in the Indian Ocean region dates back to fourth century CE.

Almost for a millennium after that, the region, which is today described as South East Asia, used to be called as Greater India. Although the southern empires like the Cholas and Pandyas had undertaken military expeditions through the great oceans to expand their influence over remote islands like Borneo and Bali, it in effect remained cultural only, to a great extent. The religion and culture of the benign colonizers were heartily welcomed by the subject societies leading to the establishment of not only the religious customs and traditions but also large temples and monuments. From Bali in Indonesia to Cham areas in Vietnam to Angkor Vat ruins in Cambodia, the living and historical evidences of the influence of India is conspicuous to this day.

History progressed, and social, political and religious realities of these lands had undergone major changes over centuries. India too was preoccupied with its battles against the invaders for almost a millennium and hence had no time for its cultural empire. Yet, the historical memories did not fade away. When the time came to unshackle from the imperialist yoke, India did not think only about itself, but the entire Asian neighbourhood. If Sri Aurobindo talked about Asian renaissance as India's historic responsibility, Gandhi and Nehru talked about Asian relations for anti-imperialist brotherhood.

In his address to a radio station in Tamil Nadu on the eve of Independence, which also happened to be his birthday, Sri Aurobindo talked about his five dreams. While advocating for freedom and unity for people of India as his first dream, Aurobindo turned to Asian resurgence as his second dream in which India had an important role to play. He exhorted:

> Asia has arisen; large parts are now quite free or are at this moment being liberated; its other still subject or partly subject parts are moving through whatever struggles towards freedom. Only a little has to be done and that will be done today or tomorrow. There, India has her part to play and has begun to play it with energy and ability which already indicate the measure of her possibilities and the place she can take in the council of the nations.[34]

[34]'1947, August 15th Message', *Sri Aurobindo Society*, http://tinyurl.com/35f995zn. Accessed on 9 January 2024.

A few months before Sri Aurobindo's exhortation came the Asian Relations Conference on 23–25 March 1947 called by Jawaharlal Nehru with the objective of bringing about a 'psychological revolution' and 'a new imagination of Asia'. There were 230 delegates and observers from 30 countries at the conference, highlighting the faith and trust reposed by many of them in India's leadership. A new 'Asianism' or 'Third Worldism' was born at the conference. Unlike the Asianism of India thus far, which was limited to the cultural remnants in Greater India, Nehru's mission was to create an Asian federation that would eventually be a step in the direction of greater world federation. Interestingly, Sri Aurobindo too talks about the same idea as his third dream a few months later.

Although Nehru declared that his intention was not 'against anybody', he and other speakers at the conference were equally categorical that the new Asianism would make sure that Asians wouldn't become the 'playthings of others'. There was a clear desire articulated by many speakers at the conference that Asia should be free of Western influences. It cannot be Communist either. Hence, the idea that Asian nations should form a coalition as Third World countries was born.

Gandhi was invited to deliver a speech on the last day of the conference. He made certain interesting observations. Terming all wise men from Zoroaster to Buddha to Jesus to Muhammad—not to talk of Rama and Krishna—to be belonging to East, Gandhi emphasized on Asia's antidotal message to the West. He said:

> What I want you to understand is the message of Asia. It is not to be learnt through the western spectacles or by imitating the atom bomb. In this age of democracy, in this age of awakening of the poorest of the poor, you

> can redeliver this message with the greatest emphasis. You will complete the conquest of the West, not through vengeance, because you have been exploited, but with real understanding. I am sanguine, if all of you put your hearts together—not merely heads—to understand the secret of the message these wise men of the East have left to us, and if we really become worthy of that great message, the conquest of the West will be completed. This conquest will be loved by the West itself.

Asian Relations Conference did not survive for long. Nehru's Asianism dream died its quiet death after the Bandung Conference of Non-Aligned nations in Indonesia in 1955. But Asianism and Third Worldism did not die. Asianism survived through different experimentations in the East Asian Summit (EAS), South Asian Association for Regional Cooperation (SAARC), Bay of Bengal Initiative for Multi-Sectoral Technical and Economic Cooperation (BIMSTEC) and Indian Ocean Rim Association (IORA). It manifested through the principle of 'Neighbourhood First' in 1990s and transformed into the principle of 'together we grow' under Prime Minister (PM) Narendra Modi. Third Worldism took the shape of non-alignment in later years and 'strategic autonomy' today.

At a time when a new Cold War is beginning to threaten the world order, India needed to turn a leaf or two from the old-world politics of Asian centrality and strategic neutrality. More importantly, it should realize that it has a much bigger role to play in the world politics than what Nehru had intended to seven decades ago.

Asianism of the last century did not succeed partly because India and China—two large nations in the region—could not get along. The Sino-Indian War of 1962 had thrown water over Indian romanticism about leading the Third World with Asian centrality. But the fact that its immediate playground is its Asian neighbourhood was never forgotten. With the formation of SAARC and BIMSTEC, it tried to return to its pet theme. It evolved further when India became a full dialogue partner with ASEAN (Association of Southeast Asian Nations) in 1995 and developed its own 'Look East policy'.

Nelson Mandela, the legendary leader of South Africa, visited India in the same year. That visit had resulted in the birth of another regional coalition called the IORA. During Atal Bihari Vajpayee's regime, the Look East policy has been upgraded into Act East policy. Through these initiatives, India tried to revive its Asianism theme. It had its Achilles heel to its west in Pakistan and by extension the Arab and Islamic Middle East and West Asia. In the last few years, PM Narendra Modi has successfully attempted to overcome the jinx and build stronger ties with that region too.

While the twentieth century ended with the collapse of the Cold War politics, the world did not remain multilateral for long. A new Cold War is taking shape in the new century with Eurasia and Indo-Pacific emerging as the epicentres of global power politics. Unlike the last century when the Cold War between the Soviet Union and the United States was fought in faraway Pacific-Atlantic region, the new Cold War is raging in India's immediate neighbourhood.

One of the central themes of the Asianism of 1940s and 1950s was that Asia wouldn't be allowed to become a playground of big power rivalry. In his Shangri La address in 2018 at Singapore, PM Modi reiterated it by insisting on Indo-pacific region to be inclusive and peaceful.[35]

---

[35]'Prime Minister's Keynote Address at Shangri la Dialogue (June 01, 2018)', *Ministry of External Affairs, Government of India*, 1 June 2018, http://tinyurl.com/4vrzva2r. Accessed on 9 January 2024.

Many Asian nations aspire for it as new war clouds gather in the region. Like at the time of budding Asianism in the last century, China remains a challenge in this region now also. During the last Cold War, China benefitted massively by siding openly with America from 1970s onwards. China's current economic prosperity is a gift of America in the 1980s and 1990s. India cannot afford such politics because the new Cold War is being fought at its doorstep. Aggression of China in the Indo-Pacific region and formation of new military alliances like Aukus led by America to counter that aggression have the potential to turn the Asian region into an Armageddon. Together, they will bring highest number of nuclear submarines in India's backyard.

India needs to recalibrate its response to this evolving challenge carefully. Western QUAD may be a romantic idea to checkmate China in UAE and Israel, but what is more important for India is the Indian Ocean region. Countries in this region look up to India as the biggest power in the neighbourhood. At the Asian Relations Conference, there were a large number of leaders present from this region and they were the most supportive of all to India's leadership. In a way, it is India's natural region of comfort.

India needs to invest more energy on this region. Its relations with immediate neighbours like Nepal, Bhutan, Myanmar, Bangladesh and Sri Lanka, with whom it shares a strong cultural and people-to-people bonds, need greater attention. China's footprints are all over in the region. India needs to go beyond its diplomats and build newer and firmer bridges with leaders and peoples in these countries.

There is a misplaced obsession with India's soft power potential in its neighbourhood among sections of Indian political establishment. It is time we realize that soft power in its conventional form is an over-used and outlived concept.

Need of the hour is smart or sharp power, where the cultural advantages are used strategically to secure national interests. Building an International Airport at the Buddhist pilgrim centre of Kushinagar in Uttar Pradesh by Modi government is one such example of smart power in action.[36]

While we should continue to benefit from our growing bonds with America and other western powers, we must never give up on the core principles of foreign policy set at the time of independence that include Asian centrality, inclusivity and strategic autonomy. While China is a 'risen power,' India is the 'rising power' in the region and if strategized well, it has the potential to play the pivotal role in building a 'world union' envisaged by Sri Aurobindo and other leaders of independence on the basis of a resurgent Asianism.

Reprinted from INDIA FOUNDATION JOURNAL, *with permission of India Foundation.*

[36]'How UP's Kushinagar International Airport Will Prove to Be a Game-Changer', *Livemint*, 20 October 2021, http://tinyurl.com/ymjwk68f. Accessed on 9 January 2024.

34

India and South Korea: Ancient Friendship Forgotten

Gimhae is an ancient city in South Korea. It was the capital of the Geumgwan Gaya kingdom—one of the three ancient kingdoms of Korea. Gaya kingdom has a historic relationship with India that goes back by more than two millennia. *Samguk yusa* (Memorabilia of the Three Kingdoms), a thirteenth century collection of legends, folktales and history of Korea's three kingdoms narrates that story.

Princess Suriratna was the daughter of King Padmasena and his wife Indumati. Padmasena was the ruler of the Kosala Kingdom in North India, with Ayodhya as the capital. According to Samguk yusa, in 48 BCE, the princess, then 16, travelled to Korea from the 'ancient land of Ayuta' and married Kim Suro, founder and King of Geumgwan Gaya in southeastern Korea.

This relationship is a cherished part of the folklore in that country. There are stories, songs and drama depicting the voyage of the princess from India to Korea. Gimhae city municipality maintains the tomb of the princess which was built atop a high mound facing the sea. Koreans believe that the princess gazes at the sea from that tomb on the high mound remembering her parents in India.

A sister-city agreement was signed between Gimhae and Ayodhya in the year 2000. Besides the tomb, Gimhae municipality has developed a nice memorial for Gandhi also. India is building a memorial for Princess Suriratna in Ayodhya.

Apart from these cultural linkages, India and South Korea share a few other commonalities. Like India, Korea also endured brutal colonization for centuries that left bitter memories. When it finally came out of the colonial yoke after World War II, it too had to endure a partition that tore it up into two parts across the 38th parallel. Both India and South Korea have hostile borders that are heavily guarded. While India faces a threat from Pakistan, South Korea faces threats from its North Korean neighbour. South Korea, like India, is a functioning liberal democracy too.

During the Korean War in 1950–53, Indian soldiers were deployed as Peace Corps as part of the UN Peace Keeping Force. Indian medical contingent—the 60th Parachute Field Ambulance—was deployed at Pyongyang in November 1950 under the command of Lt Col Rangaraj. It was the last to leave what was to become North Korea in 1953. The American soldiers, who were fighting against the North Korean and Chinese armies, were retreating to the South when they found the team of Indian Army Medical Corps jawans still stuck in the North. They asked the Indians to leave behind all medical equipment and retreat with them. But the Indian contingent refused. Amid heavy bombing, they collected medical supplies and loaded them into the wagons of an abandoned Japanese train. Luckily, a couple of jawans knew how to run a train engine. They brought all their men and medical supplies back to safety using that train. The engine that the jawans drove back stands at the border as a tourist attraction.

India headed the Neutral Nations Repatriation Commission (NNRC) and was entrusted with the responsibility of overseeing the partition of Korea in 1953 that included the safe transfer of prisoners of war. Lt Gen. K.S. Thimmayya was appointed

Chairman of the Commission with Maj. Gen. S.S.P. Thorat assisting him. The custodian forces of India arrived in July 1953. Praising India's handling of the ceasefire and subsequent partition, renowned British philosopher Bertrand Russel wrote: 'In the two matters, the mediation of India made it possible for agreements to be reached. A great deal of courage was needed since each side was angry whenever any concession was made to the other, so that the pursuit of even-handed justice led to unpopularity with East and West alike. For my part, I thought the decisions of the Indian authorities as regards Korea came as near to impartiality as is possible.'

Talking of the partition, Koreans were less lucky as the border between the two countries was declared as a demilitarized zone (DMZ) by the UN in 1953 and a contingent of over 30,000 foreign soldiers continue to guard it. The four-km wide DMZ, the only such border in the world, divides North and South Korea. Although a multinational force, 90 per cent of the soldiers come from the US military only, effectively placing the border control in the hands of America. It is the most heavily guarded border in the world. Thousands of soldiers of both countries lined both sides of the border alongside heavy artillery, rockets and other weapons.

But South Koreans are deeply committed to the unification of both Koreas. There is a Ministry of Unification in the South Korean government. Two decades ago, when the relations between the two sides were better, the rich South Korean government took the initiative of establishing Kaesong Industrial Complex on the North Korean side of the DMZ in 2004. More than 120 South Korean companies started operations in Kaesong providing employment to more than 50,000 North Korean workers. This goodwill gesture from the South was to help the North earn foreign currency besides providing jobs to the workers.

The industrial park functioned well for more than a decade until tensions returned between the two sides with the rise of Kim Jong Un to power in Pyongyang. The industrial area was completely shut in 2016.

South Korea uses border tourism to showcase its commitment to peace and unification. One can go inside the DMZ to see the border line and also the ghost city of Kaesong using binoculars from the South Korean side. When the relations soured in the last decade, a 'flag post war' erupted between the two sides. The South Koreans hoisted their national flag on the border and the North challenged it by hoisting their flag on a taller pole. This competition went on until the North raised its pole height to 160 metres and the South decided to give up. Using the binoculars, one can see both the flags and also a huge and provocative slogan etched on the hills by the North claiming 'Our country is the best'.

One interesting aspect in this border drama is the 'cow bridge' inside the DMZ. This bridge that connects two sides has an interesting history. Chung Ju-yung, the owner of Hyundai Motors, one of the South Korean behemoths, was originally from a poor family in North Korea. Chung's father was a farmer. He had a few cattle, one of which he asked his son Jung to sell in the market to arrange for his daughter's wedding. Jung sold the cow and fled to Seoul with that money. Always interested in doing something bigger than agriculture, Jung started a car repair workshop, which eventually became the Hyundai Motor Company.

This rags-to-riches story doesn't end here. Jung wanted to pay back to his family and also the country. In 1993, he became the first person from the South in 40 years to enter North Korea. He crossed DMZ to meet his father. With him were 1,001 cows, of which 1,000 cows were gifted to poor farmers in the North and one returned to his father.[37]

South Koreans continue to cherish that goodwill for their counterparts in the North. There were huge celebrations when the North Korean athletes came to Seoul to participate in the Winter Olympics in 2018. Both teams marched together under the Korean Unification Flag during the opening ceremony of the games. North Korean supreme leader Kim Jong Un sent a high-level delegation led by his firebrand sister Kim Yo Jong. She met South Korean President Moon Jae-in at the inaugural ceremony and shook hands with him. It was the first time after the Korean War that the leaders of the two countries at the highest level met directly.

Relations between the two Koreas deteriorated in the last few years once again. South has moved closer to the US by allowing for the deployment of the US-made THAAD (Terminal High Altitude Area Defense) anti-missile system in 2017. It is being wooed by the US to join the mega semiconductor manufacturing and supply chain alliance called Chip 4. The current government led by conservative President Yoon Suk Yeol is openly tilted towards the US to the chagrin of China. Relations between South Korea and China, despite bilateral trade being the highest at 300 billion dollars, have become sour and uneasy.

South Korean economy is booming. Its democracy is thriving. Its society is progressive and open. Its history has many commonalities with India. All this should catapult India–South Korea relations to greater heights. Right now, the bilateral trade stands at a meagre 23 billion dollars, one-thirteenth of China. Indian immigrant population too is just 15,000 whereas the Chinese immigrants are more than six lakhs.

---

[37]Brooke, James, 'A Suicide and Uncertainty in Korea', *The New York Times*, 7 August 2023, http://tinyurl.com/4y4sa6zd. Accessed on 9 January 2024.

India enjoys goodwill among ordinary Koreans. Its businesses in India—Hyundai, Samsung, Kia, LG and POSCO are thriving. The BTS, the most popular K-pop group in Korea, is a massive hit among youth in India, especially in the Northeast. Yet the relationship remains low-key. Its potential calls for greater people-to-people initiatives besides governments' diplomatic efforts.

Reprinted from CHINTAN–INDIA FOUNDATION BLOGS, with permission of India Foundation.

35

India Is Playing Its Geo-Strategic Cards Effectively

The diligence, dexterity and determination that Prime Minister (PM) Narendra Modi has displayed in diplomacy in the last few years and the immense geo-strategic costs that he has inflicted on India's traditional rivals, is an important chapter. India's handling of the stand-off with China in the last few months (as of September 2020) along the Line of Actual Control (LAC) is one such example, widely talked about in the diplomatic circles today with awe and admiration.

China has been a difficult neighbour. It has quietly reframed its neighbourhood policy in the last few years. In 2003, Premier Wen Jiabao articulated 'Good Neighbourhood, Secure Neighbourhood, and Wealthy Neighbourhood' as China's neighbourhood vision. In 2009, President Hu Jintao talked about his vision of 'periphery diplomacy' for a 'harmonious world'. But President Xi Jinping has introduced an aggressive policy with China's neighbours since 2013 that involved expanding cultural influence, improving regional security cooperation and socializing in the region to make countries accept China's view of its core interests, and enforcing China's sovereignty and territorial claims.

Not many could stand up to this aggression. In the South and East China Sea areas, China unilaterally enforced the nine-dash line maritime boundary, while neighbours like Japan, the Philippines, Vietnam, Malaysia and Indonesia watched helplessly. In a landmark verdict, the United Nations Convention on the Law of the Sea (UNCLOS) on 12 July 2016, decried China's historical claims based on the nine-dash line. But China simply rejected the verdict. The petitioner, the Philippines, couldn't do much. It couldn't do much either when its ships were harassed by the Chinese Coast Guard in the same area later. Vietnam had to be content with international condemnation when their fishing vessel was forcefully sunk by the Chinese Coast Guard. Recently, a Chinese survey ship, Haiyang Dizhi, encroached deep inside the Malaysian exclusive economic zone in search of oil reserves, while the Malaysians were forced to look the other way. Even the Americans and the Japanese find it difficult to counter the aggression of the People's Liberation Army Navy (PLAN) in the South and East China Sea. Their ships are regularly accosted, many times by moving dangerously close, by PLA naval warships. The aircraft carriers of the PLAN, like the Liaoning, undertake exercises in close vicinity of the American carriers provocatively.

But one place where China finds the going tough nowadays is on the Indo-Tibetan border along the LAC. Its aggressive manoeuvres are met with stiff resistance from the Indian side. The first taste of India's proportional response to the aggression came at the Doklam tri-junction in North Sikkim in 2017. Indian resistance forced the Chinese to backtrack. A similar proportional response is being offered by the Indian forces along the LAC in Ladakh in the last couple of months. The Indian response in the form of 'proactive diplomacy and strong ground posturing' has forced China to alter its approach. India is continuing its efforts to restore peace in the region.

Meanwhile, PM Modi's proactive diplomacy with the countries in the Arab world has led to the 57-nation

Organization of Islamic Cooperation (OIC) shedding its anti-India rhetoric. A virtual split seems imminent in the OIC between the Arab and non-Arab countries. The Arab world is led by Saudi Arabia, while Turkey and Pakistan are playing an active role in mobilizing non-Arab Muslim states. Sensing the potential geo-strategic damage from the impending split in the OIC, China stepped in extending tacit support to the emerging new Islamic alliance. Prime Minister Mahathir Mohamad of Malaysia hosted a conference of the non-Arab Muslim countries in Kuala Lumpur. Turkish President Recep Tayyip Erdogan played an important role in this conference. With a view to sabotage the conference, the Saudis used their financial clout with Pakistan to force PM Imran Khan to abstain. Khan had to succumb to Saudi pressure. China stepped in to rescue Pakistan from the crisis, thus paving the way for a non-Saudi-led alliance of the Islamic states.

India has played its geo-strategic cards very effectively through this entire process. It has even isolated China at the UN Security Council on two occasions in the last one year when it tried to push through a discussion over Kashmir at the behest of Pakistan. A diligent handling of the situation by India's Permanent Representative helped in thwarting these moves, leaving China red-faced. In the latest instance, in August this year, China couldn't secure support from any country except Niger, when it tried to initiate a discussion on Kashmir. Pakistan's efforts to get some innocent Indians sanctioned by the United Nations Security Council (UNSC) as international terrorists too came a cropper due to India's proactive diplomacy. Besides the US, several European nations like the UK and France came out quickly to block Pakistani mischief with tacit Chinese support.

So far, it has been a successful run for India. The delicate, yet effective strategic moves by PM Modi had given rich dividends. But India should be prepared for certain new challenges ahead. Turkey is taking over as the Chair of the United Nations in September 2020. The ECOSOC, an important UN body on social and economic affairs, has Pakistan as the elected president. While India cherished its historical relations with Turkey, tensions between the countries remained a feature of the relationship primarily due to Turkey's intimate bond with Pakistan. On Kashmir, Turkey has largely sided with Pakistan in the past, although Erdogan has tried to slightly moderate the position.

However, with China raring to get back at India at all international forums and its not-so-tacit efforts at propping up the Turkey-Pakistan-Malaysia leadership to counter the Saudi-led OIC, issues such as Islamophobia and Kashmir may return to dominate the international discourse. The new OIC led by the troika will be headquartered at New York.

India should be prepared for this new face-off at the UN. The US, with elections around the corner, will be less interested in these affairs for some time. India's traditional allies in Europe will help, but it needs to cultivate countries like Australia, Vietnam and Japan in the Indo-Pacific neighbourhood to tackle this new challenge.

36

The Indonesian Example for Indian Muslims

Wokes are the greatest enemy of classical liberalism. Their championing of the hijab cause is a great disservice to women of Islam who fought countless battles for centuries to unshackle themselves from the harsh Islamic patriarchal yoke. By deploying deceptive vocabulary like choice and freedom, and demonstrating false camaraderie with a few misled Muslim girls, wokes are actually pushing women back into the same orthodoxy that has been the bane of their lives.

But the opponents, who are taking to the streets against the hijab, are also not doing any great service. They are harming the larger cause by converting this essentially intra-religion battle into an unnecessary inter-religious war. Instead of leaving the discipline question to government authorities and encouraging voices from within the gender and community, they chose to pit saffron scarves against hijabs, not realizing that such you-me dichotomy will only weaken the reformist endeavour within society in general, and Islam in particular.

After all, women of different civilizations and religions had to battle it out for dignity and equality in different periods in history. In Hinduism, continuous reform, aided by government and public leadership, has resulted in a marked improvement in the condition of women.

In Islam, too, such a battle against medieval orthodoxy is ongoing in different countries. A number of Islamic countries, with an exception to the ones like Iran and Afghanistan, have disallowed mandatory imposition of the hijab. Some Islamic liberals point out that the hijab in Islam was not about covering the head and body but about modesty in dress. But woke liberals insist that bikini and burqa are representative of a woman's choice.

Islamist orthodoxy, that makes the lives of women, minorities and non-believers miserable, is essentially a product of the West Asian Wahhabi tradition. It is this regressive, puritanical and often violent version of Islam that has spread to India and other parts of South Asia, besides taking hold in several Arab and North African countries. It imposed medieval customs and spawned terrorism and violence in countries wherever it went.

In India, the Deobandi school largely favoured Wahhabism. Of late, the south Indian state of Kerala has emerged as the hotbed of radical Islam. Wahhabism came to Kerala along with the money that the immigrants brought, resulting in more and more madrassas and mosques preaching the fundamentalist version of Islam. Political movements like the Popular Front of India and its affiliates like the Social Democratic Party of India are actively promoting this radical and patriarchal Islam. Medieval practices like chopping off the hands of people accused of imagined blasphemy, imposing head-to-toe burqa on Muslim girls and women, and promoting ill-devised activities like love jihad are all the result of this malice spreading fast in the state and the neighbourhood. These very forces were behind the recent hijab controversy in coastal Karnataka too.

Countering this medieval Wahhabi Islam should be an important obligation for the Muslim leadership in India. A new 'Look East' policy in religion may help in this endeavour.

While West Asian Islam is struggling to get out of the stranglehold of the Wahhabi interpretation, a new movement for Eastern and humanitarian Islam is taking root in our eastern neighbourhood in Indonesia. That movement, led by the country's largest Muslim religious organization known as Nahdlatul Ulama (NU), is worth noting and emulating for Indian Muslims.

With a population of 240 million, Indonesia is the world's largest Islamic country. Its Islam, with minor aberrations like the Aceh province, remained essentially Javanese and syncretic. Both the political and Islamic leadership in Indonesia has made scrupulous efforts to keep Wahhabism at arm's length and nurtured the Sufi version of Islam which is tolerant, pluralist and liberal. When the country declared independence in 1945, the constitution had called it a multi-religious and pluralistic nation with the motto: *Bhinneka Tunggal Ika* (oneness amid diversity). Since then, the NU has ensured that the shadow of medieval Islam did not come to influence Muslim behaviour in the country.

I had the opportunity to meet with the NU leadership in 2018 when I was invited to speak at a conference hosted by them in Yogyakarta. I also had the opportunity to meet with Yahya Cholil Staquf, popularly known as Pak Yahya, the influential general secretary of the NU. The NU is a body with a membership of over 90 million Indonesian Muslims, making it the world's largest Muslim body. In my hour-long interaction, I was impressed with Pak Yahya's open-mindedness and reformist zeal.

Later that year, I was forwarded an article written by Pak Yahya in *The Daily Telegraph* with the title 'How can we prevent another atrocity like the one in Christchurch?' The 'Christchurch atrocity' that Pak Yahya referred to was the shooting incident that had taken place in Christchurch in

New Zealand in March 2019 in which a Christian zealot had entered a mosque on a Friday and massacred more than 50 innocent Muslim worshippers.

Usually in such articles, it is expected that the author would harangue readers about Islamophobia and victimization of Muslims in the Western world. But Pak Yahya's article was refreshingly different. In an introspective tone, he says:

> [There is an urgent need to address the] problematic elements of Islamic orthodoxy that underlie the Islamist worldview, fuelling violence on both sides. Jihadist doctrine, goals and strategy can be traced to specific tenets of orthodox, authoritative Islam and its historic practice… those portions of Shariah that promote Islamic supremacy, encourage enmity towards non-Muslims and require the establishment of a caliphate. It is these elements—still taught by most Sunni and Shia institutions—that constitute a summons to perpetual conflict.

Putting forth a rather courageous argument, Pak Yahya even cautions against the 'weaponising of the term Islamophobia', and insists that 'in reality, it is the spread of Islamist extremism and terror that primarily contributes to the rise of Islamophobia throughout the non-Muslim world.'

The NU, under successive leaders in the last few years, has been spearheading campaigns to champion a version of Islam that promotes peace and pluralism. In 2016, it hosted the International Summit of Moderate Islamic Leaders (ISOMIL). In 2017, it invited more than 300 international religious scholars to deliberate on the 'obsolete tenets of classical Islamic law' which promote 'perpetual conflict with those who do not embrace or submit to Islam.'

In the ISOMIL summit in 2016, the NU had come out with a 'Declaration on Humanitarian Islam'. 'If Muslims do not address the key tenets of Islamic orthodoxy that authorize and explicitly enjoin… violence, anyone—at any time—may harness the orthodox teachings of Islam to defy what they claim to be the illegitimate laws and authority of an infidel state and butcher their fellow citizens, regardless of whether they live in the Islamic world or the West,' it explicitly states.

What Islam needs today is *ijtihad*—a process of making legal decisions in Islamic law through independent reasoning. Wahhabi Islam is incapable of that as it is stuck in medieval interpretations of the religion. Its insistence on *fiqh*—the medieval human understanding of the divine Islamic injunctions—results in situations that parts of India face today in the form of the hijab controversy. It is this archaic interpretation of the fiqh that is responsible for the crisis in Muslim-non-Muslim relations, and the rise in orthodoxy and terrorism in the name of Islam. It is this understanding of Islam that promotes concepts like al-ummat and al-khilafat. This discrepancy can be addressed only through Eastern Islam represented by organizations like the NU.

The NU has a clear policy of rejection of many such Wahhabi influences. It is against state support to the Wahhabi ideology. It demands that Muslims accept the authority of the nation state in which they live and give up demands for special treatment under Sharia laws or other customs of the past. '*Hubbul Wathan Minal Iman* (Patriotism is integral to the Islamic faith),' is its policy. 'Increasingly, Muslims' behaviour patterns reflect an obsession with the formal aspects of religion. This has led to the widespread phenomenon of outwardly religious people with corrupt souls,' the declaration bemoans, hinting at the return of practices like the hijab.

'The Humanitarian Islam movement is dedicated to facilitating the emergence of societal consensus, among Muslims and non-Muslims alike, to depoliticize the issue of

Islam, and prevent the abuse of religion to promote sectarian hatred, supremacism and violence,' the declaration concludes. I heard the delightful news that the NU has recently elected its most progressive leader Pak Yahya as its new chairman. Pak Yahya enjoys the support of the Indonesian government and President Joko Widodo.

It is important to understand that while in battlefields, swords will be met with swords, in the battlefield of religions, fundamentalist dogmas must be countered not with another kind of fundamentalism but progressive reform. The NU in Indonesia shows the way for that reform.

NEW REALITIES AND CHALLENGES

'Democracy disciplined and enlightened is the finest thing in the world. A democracy prejudiced, ignorant, superstitious, will land itself in chaos and may be self-destroyed.'[38]

—MAHATMA GANDHI

[38]'True Democracy', *Bombay Sarvodaya Mandal & Gandhi Research Foundation*, http://tinyurl.com/py6fk6cd. Accessed on 20 December 2023.

37

Beware Zombie Democracy

India needs to be wary of the new authoritarianism creeping across the world.

Disasters, natural or man-made, have consequences. A hundred years ago, a pandemic came riding on the devastation caused by World War I, leading to the destabilization of the world order of the new nation states. The Great Depression of the 1930s had added fuel to the fire. The result was a decade of threatening communist and fascist authoritarianism across Europe, culminating in World War II and great human suffering.

Out of this struggle and suffering rose democracies in large parts of the world after the end of World War II. When countries with huge population like India opted for democracy, many more nations were encouraged to follow the bandwagon. By the end of the last century, more than 120 countries became functional democracies, including some from the erstwhile Soviet empire.

The Soviet constitution had a provision for republics to secede through a popular mandate. Nobody had dared to invoke it when Stalin, Khrushchev and Brezhnev were at the helm. But Mikhail Gorbachev had lit the fire by allowing free elections, and it became a wildfire engulfing the entire Soviet Union. One of the first to exploit it was Boris Yeltsin. Yeltsin was elected chairman of the Russian republic in 1990.

When Gorbachev was put under house arrest by his own comrades in 1991, Yeltsin seized the opportunity from the reigning chaos and declared independence for Russia from the Soviet Union. The rest is history. The Soviet Union had collapsed like a pack of cards with republic after republic holding elections and declaring independence. The democratic fever had reached its peak when Vladimir Putin, whom Yeltsin had declared his successor in 1999, said that 'history has proven that all dictatorships, all authoritarian forms of government, are transient. Only democratic systems are intransient.'

The collapse of the Soviet authoritarian regime together with the rise of democracies in almost all parts of the world had convinced Western scholars like Francis Fukuyama to conclude that the era of authoritarianism was over. 'End of history,' they screamed, and declared that the liberal democratic model was the only panacea for the future of mankind.

As the world was settling for democracy as the credible way, there came the rise of Islamic terrorism, followed by the economic debacle of 2008–10 that had wiped out the wealth of many nations and individuals. Economic downturn, Islamist aggression, terrorism and social inequalities had pushed the democratic world on the back foot.

The Covid-19 pandemic has hastened that process further. The monumental human costs of the pandemic have pushed people more and more into the hands of governments in desperation. States with efficient systems and responsive public institutions have been able to manage the pandemic well, whereas those with built-in inefficiency failed miserably. In either scenario, people's helplessness has been exploited by leaders usurping more powers and turning authoritarian in varied degrees. The world is once again witnessing with dismay the setting in of a democratic deficit and the return of the demons of dictatorship of the last century.

Xi Jinping is leading the charge of communist authoritarianism with the misleading motto that authoritarianism with efficiency were better than dysfunctional and incompetent democracies. Many seem to be falling for it.

All communists are authoritarian, but not all authoritarians need to be communists. In Russia, Putin began his career in 1999 on the anti-communist plank. But within a few years, he started invoking Ilyin as the role model for Russia. Ilyin (Vladimir Ilin) was also the pen name of Lenin, whose middle name was Ilyich. But the Ilyin that Putin was referring to was not a communist. He was the fascist philosopher of the last century, Ivan Ilyin. 'The principle of democracy is the irresponsible human atom,' declared Ilyin, adding 'we must reject the mechanical and arithmetical understanding of politics' as well as 'blind faith in the number of votes'. He attempted facetiously to equate fascism with patriotism and claimed that it was nothing but the 'redemptive excess of patriotic arbitrariness'.

Ilyin died in Switzerland in 1954, unmourned in Soviet Russia for his anti-Bolshevik fascism. But Putin intends to resurrect him. He was reburied in Moscow in 2005 under Putin's gaze. Putin spoke about him often, inside the Duma and outside. His shenanigans are projecting Ilyin as the philosopher of Russia's future. It suits Putin because Ilyin, in true fascist tradition, talked about a 'redeemer' who would be a godsend and save Russia from the communists on one hand and the West on the other.

Many countries in the world are coming under the influence of either version of authoritarianism. An era of 'managed' or 'guided' democracies seems to have begun. Kenneth Roth, the executive director of Human Rights Watch, calls them 'Zombie Democracies', where the 'leaders have held periodic elections to enhance their legitimacy but monopolized the media, restricted civil society, and manipulated state institutions and resources to ensure that they remained in power'.

Communist regimes like North Korea, Cuba and Vietnam, or for that matter the Islamist autocracies like Saudi Arabia and the UAE do not pretend to follow any democratic principle. Several regimes in Central Asia, the West Asia and Africa are also openly and unapologetically authoritarian. But it is the zombie democracies that are throwing up Ilyin-inspired pretenders from Hungary and Belarus in Eastern Europe to Venezuela and Nicaragua in the Western hemisphere.

Two democracies, the oldest and the largest—the US and India—have thus far been able to largely avoid this trend, although they too occasionally demonstrated their vulnerability. Indira Gandhi's infamous Emergency of 1975–77 was the darkest phase of Indian democracy while the US had in Donald Trump a president who took the country almost to the brink. However, societies in both countries demonstrated vigilance and dynamism to overcome those authoritarian challenges and restore the liberal credentials of their democracies.

Democracies in the West have come a long distance. It took more than two centuries for American democracy to mature. It had its first Black president after 220 years while a woman president is still awaited. Britain, too, struggled to balance monarchy, aristocracy and democracy in its political system. That was the reason why both Winston Churchill and Clement Attlee had reacted with scepticism when the Indian leadership declared its intention to opt for parliamentary democracy after Independence.

There were domestic sceptics too, but Nehru categorically declared that 'obviously we are aiming at democracy and nothing less than a democracy'. India proved all those sceptics wrong by building a vibrant democratic model in just seven decades after Independence.

Democracy, like any other political model, thrives only in the right environment. B.R. Ambedkar, in his famous concluding address, popularly known as the 'Three Warnings Speech', to the Constituent Assembly of India as the Chairman of the Drafting Committee, on 25 November 1949, attributed it to the age-old ethos of India. He said:

> It is not that India did not know what is democracy. There was a time when India was studded with republics, and even where there were monarchies, they were either elected or limited. They were never absolute. It is not that India did not know Parliaments or Parliamentary Procedure. A study of the Buddhist Bhikshu Sanghas discloses that not only there were Parliaments—for, the Sanghas were nothing but Parliaments—but the Sanghas knew and observed all the rules of Parliamentary Procedure known to modern times. They had rules regarding seating arrangements, rules regarding Motions, Resolutions, Quorum, Whip, Counting of Votes, Voting by Ballot, Censure Motion, Regularization, Res Judicata, etc. Although these rules of Parliamentary Procedure were applied by the Buddha to the meetings of the Sanghas, he must have borrowed them from the rules of the Political Assemblies functioning in the country in his time.

Deendayal Upadhyaya, the leading light of the opposition Bharatiya Jana Sangh at the time, had added that the 'Vedic Sabhas and Samitis were also organised on the basis of democracy, and many medieval states in India were completely democratic. We have confined the powers and privileges of kings and made them cater to the demands of the public.'

The architects of the Constitution of India—Nehru and Patel to Ambedkar and Rajendra Prasad—were all committed democrats. So were other leaders like Gandhi and Upadhyaya. While those in the Constituent Assembly like Nehru and Ambedkar were influenced largely by Western models of democracy, Gandhi and Upadhyaya drew their inspiration from Indian experience. Together, they built strong foundations for India's democracy by embellishing the Western democratic edifice with quintessential Indian wisdom and strong moralism.

Gandhi and Deendayal Upadhyaya did not endorse the majoritarian streak in Western democracies. Upadhyaya insisted:

> Democracy is not merely the rule of the majority. In a majoritarian government there will at least be one segment of the public whose voice has been stifled even though it may be right. This form of democracy cannot work for everyone's welfare and good. Therefore, in any form of democracy in India, election, majority and minority, all must be combined and harmonized at one pace. Anyone, who has a different opinion from the majority, even if he is a single individual, his viewpoint must be respected and incorporated into the governance.

Gandhi, too, echoed similar sentiments in his writings in *Young India* repeatedly. He wrote:

> The rule of majority has a narrow application, i.e., one should yield to the majority in matters of detail. But it is slavery to be amenable to the majority, no matter what its decisions are. Democracy is not a state in which people act like sheep. Under democracy, individual liberty of opinion and action is jealously guarded. I, therefore, believe that the minority has a perfect right to act differently from the majority [...] The rule of majority, when it becomes coercive, is as intolerable as that of a bureaucratic minority.

Gandhi and Ambedkar represented two different spectrums of the political opinion at the time of the making of Indian democracy. But both had similar concerns with regard to its success. Gandhi's insistence was that democracy should become the 'sovereignty of the people based on pure moral authority'. Ambedkar warned that reneging on constitutional means and resorting to British-era tactics like non-cooperation, resorting to hero-worship and ignoring social democracy would surely lead to its downfall.

Both Gandhi and Ambedkar were responding to the experiences of their time—for Gandhi, democracy meant the weak getting the same chance as the strong. For Ambedkar, it was about giving voice to the voiceless.

For democracies to succeed, Gandhi and Ambedkar believed that parliamentary majorities needed to be restrained through constitutional ethics and public morality. Enlightened public opinion is critical to democracy's success. Julius Caesar's story is a case in point to understand the nature of unenlightened public opinion. When Brutus murdered Caesar, the Roman public celebrated it. But when Mark Antony revealed Brutus' deception, they went after Brutus. 'It is difficult to keep democracy alive between the two forms of government—mobocracy and autocracy,' Deendayal Upadhyaya averred.

India has demonstrated in the last seven decades that the political morality of its citizens has been robust. Its keepers were not the political class but influential public institutions and organizations like the Rashtriya Swayamsevak Sangh (RSS), the media and other civil society institutions. Their power was on display at the time of Emergency. When Indira Gandhi decided to revoke Emergency in March 1977, she did not anticipate the severe rebuke that she would get at the hands of the Indian electorate. It was so harsh that both she and her son had lost their elections to Parliament in 1977.

This enlightened public opinion had sailed Indian democracy through fractured mandates, coalition experiments and short-lived governments to the stable, full-majority regime of the present, each time testing the mettle and steadfastness of its leaders. When the leaders were found wanting, it did not hesitate to change them.

It is nobody's claim that democracies are perfect political systems. Churchill used to quip that democracy was the worst form of government 'except for all the others'. Nehru held the same opinion: 'Democracy is good. I say this because other systems are worse. So we are forced to accept democracy. It has good points and also bad. But merely saying that democracy will solve all the problems is utterly wrong. Problems are solved by intelligence and hard work.'

Zombie-ization is a real threat that all countries in the democratic world are facing today. The vulnerabilities of democracy can be exploited if the rulers are selfish and the ruled foolish. After all, as Timothy Snyder pointed out in his book *The Road to Unfreedom*, 'what robber would not prefer to be called a redeemer'. That is what is leading to the spectre of authoritarianism looming over many democracies. It could only be 'transient' as Putin pointed out two decades ago. Yet, it would cause huge devastation as witnessed in the last century.

Such an eventuality can be averted by functioning democracies like America and India coming to the aid of the weltering ones. The sad reality, though, is that it was the Nixon-Kissinger duo who had legitimized Mao's autocracy in the 1970s while George H.W. Bush was desperately appealing to the Soviet republics not to destroy the Union in the 1990s. While they lectured fellow democracies like India on human rights and civic freedoms, from Ronald Reagan to Trump, the US unabashedly sided with autocrats and authoritarians in the Middle East and elsewhere.

Democracies can survive only when leaders scrupulously adhere to constitutional ethics. It is about respecting constitutional order, conventions and public institutions. The Americans have a written constitution, the British don't. Yet both developed healthy conventions that safeguard their democracies. There is a beautiful convention in the US of the outgoing president leaving behind a handwritten letter for the incoming one which the new incumbent of the White House would get to see on the first day in the Oval office. 'We are just temporary occupants of this office. That makes us guardians of those democratic institutions and traditions—like rule of law, separation of powers, equal protection, and civil liberties...Regardless of the push and pull of daily politics, it's up to us to leave those instruments of our democracy at least as strong as we found them,' Barack Obama wrote in his letter to Trump in January 2017.

As India celebrated its 75th year of independence, this history, this present and these warnings are as much relevant to it as to any other democracy.

Reprinted from OPEN MAGAZINE, with permission of Open Media Network Pvt. Ltd.

38

The Liberal Waterloo

By destroying everything between the individual and the state, neoliberals have signed their own death warrant. Two historic events that took place around the same time towards the end of eighteenth century made the US and France the motherships of liberalism in the world. The first was the making of the American constitution that came into effect on 4 March 1789. Liberal ideas of individualism, freedom, equality and human rights became the founding ideas of the American constitution, a product of *The Federalist Papers* of James Madison, Alexander Hamilton and the lesser known John Jay. The second historic event happened some 6,000 km away in feudal France. A popular revolution broke out on 5 May 1789 on the streets of Paris, leading to the deposition of the centuries-old ancient regime led by King Louis XVI. Famously known as the French Revolution, this historic event, although survived only for a decade, established a constitutional government in France and laid strong foundations for a liberal democratic order based on the famous principles of liberty, equality and fraternity.

Both America and France emerged as beacons of liberal constitutionalism in the world in the last two centuries. They genuinely prided over their liberal credentials and successfully transported those ideas into almost all continents. Of the three great ideas of Western origin—liberalism, conservatism and communism—liberalism acquired greater halo and became a legitimate universal political idea of the last century. The French Revolution's tri-ideals of liberty, equality and fraternity inspired and gave birth to many liberal democracies in the world, including India. For the Americans, the essence of their liberal dogma lies in the First Amendment, adopted as a part of the ten Amendments—famously known as the Bill of Rights—on 15 December 1791. The First Amendment is the epitome of the freedoms that Americans enjoy today—freedom of religion, speech, media, assembly and freedom to petition.

Every idea has a shelf life. The Marxian idea of communism met its Waterloo in the last century. When the collapse of communism happened towards the end of the last century and the conservative ideas of religion, morals and social structures too were sufficiently vilified with enormous zeal, the liberal elite in the West started dreaming of unassailability of their liberal bandwagon. Some of them even pronounced the 'end of history'. Western liberalism was declared as the singular panacea for mankind's future.

But the first two decades of the twenty-first century appear to be shaking up the foundations of that grand Western liberal idea too. In country after country, the liberals themselves are taking to streets now, demanding that those liberal ideas be damned. Democracy, once cherished by the liberals as the cornerstone of liberal constitutionalism, is today regarded as a wobbling bogey producing populist authoritarians and dictatorial demagogues. In smaller countries like Bolivia, Peru, Kyrgyzstan and many others, the citizens took to the streets in recent times against the election results. In Belarus, the protests against the re-election of President Alexander Lukashenko are ongoing. In several of these popular protests against the elected regimes, the liberals seem to be leading the march.

Right from the time of Plato and Aristotle, democracy has been seen as an imperfect yet the best available form of popular will. Democracies have matured over centuries and produced responsible and influential leaders across many countries. The liberals cheered the rise of leaders like Roosevelt, Kennedy, Clinton and Barack Obama, while the conservatives too had their own applause reserved for an Eisenhower, a Reagan, a Thatcher or a Merkel. But that bipartisan appreciation of the democratic virtue seems passé now. The liberal intellectuals appear convinced that their pet theme has passed its prime. They are convinced that Plato and Aristotle to Alexis de Tocqueville were right in their scepticism about democracy. The liberal onslaught over it today is most vicious, but also most vacuous.

What went wrong? Why are the liberals so annoyed with their own ideals now? Why the liberal democracies that they themselves nurtured look illiberal to them, producing populists and authoritarians? Why do neoliberals now come to hate the very classical ideas of liberalism that include the spirit of the First Amendment? Simply put, why are liberals against liberalism?

The immediate cause appears to be the rise of nationalist leaders in the world using liberal democratic institutions. The return of nationalism as the flavour of the season in the twenty-first century is unsettling to neoliberals. The 'democratic competence' of ordinary people, once regarded as the foundation for the liberal order, is now portrayed as questionable. Facebook and X (formerly Twitter), pompously declared not long ago as the voices of the faceless millions, are now seen as the dangerous vehicles of Trumpian illiberalism. Liberal demigods like John Stuart Mill are being pulled out of the library shelves and dusted off to proclaim that 'persons of genius', a class that both Plato and Mill considered fit to be the ruling class—Plato called them 'philosopher kings'—ought to be brought back.

Something is wrong with neoliberals. They are now vociferous against the very core liberal ideas of universal franchise and unfettered freedom of expression. Classical liberalism was not bad. It was a non-partisan project committed according to dignity and liberty to the individuals. Towards that end, it sought to minimize the role of the government and allow for individual enterprise to be the motivating engine for social progress. Such liberal ideas are not new to the non-Western world either. Dignity and liberty of the individual were regarded as the sacred goal by the ancient Indian classical thought. Bhishma's Dharma Rajya to Gandhi's Ram Rajya epitomized human dignity and freedom. Just as Eastern liberalism owed its existence and rise to its religion, morals and corresponding institutions, Western liberalism, too, benefitted from its philosophers and religions like Christianity.

If Western liberalism came to this pass today, the liberals are to be blamed. While the classical liberal ideals needed institutions to nurture and flourish, the neoliberals have done just the opposite. Everything between the individual and the state, including religion, morals and social institutions have been destroyed by the overzealous liberal elite. The result is before the world today in the form of a death warrant for neoliberalism.

What comes after this? The thinking world has to seriously ponder this question. Liberal democracies had stabilized in the world after World War II. Neoliberals have distorted them. That should not pave the way for the return of the feudalists and fascists. Classical liberal ideals of human dignity and freedom must be upheld and protected. But they need a new expression in the twenty-first century. A search for a new vehicle for that purpose is the need of the hour. More than ideologies, idealism and pragmatism should drive such a quest.

(*This is not exactly a review of any one book. But one latest book that I read*—Why Liberalism Failed—*has triggered these thoughts in me. The book by Patrick Deneen is very thought-provoking and a cogent critique of modern liberal fault-lines.*)

Reprinted from OPEN MAGAZINE, *with permission of Open Media Network Pvt. Ltd.*

39

The Trap of Victimhood Politics

On 30 October 2021, Prime Minister (PM) Narendra Modi met Pope Francis at the Vatican, a meeting that Modi called 'very warm', and the Vatican described as 'cordial'. The PM later tweeted that he had invited the Pope to visit India and the Ministry of External Affairs confirmed that the Pope had accepted.

This should simply be seen as a meeting between the PM of India and the head of a religious order that boasts the second-largest following in the country. The Pope is not a 'head of state' in the conventional sense nor does the United Nations (UN) recognize him as one. Under the Lateran Treaty, a purely bilateral one entered in 1929, King Victor Emanuel of Italy had granted the Vatican independent status. It has neither separate citizenship nor any formal government.

What was admitted at the UN in 1948 as a 'non-member state' with only an observer status was not the Vatican but the 'Holy See'. The Holy See is the supreme governing body of Catholic churches over the world. The Pope is designated as its head, not through any political process but under canon law. The Vatican City is regarded only as the 'vassal' territory of the Holy See.

That being the reality, not one but two Bharatiya Janata Party (BJP) PMs had visited the Vatican and welcomed the Pope to India. Atal Bihari Vajpayee had visited the Vatican in

June 2000. A year before, in November 1999, his government facilitated a visit by Pope John Paul II to India, in which the Pope gave a controversial call: 'Just as the first millennium saw the cross firmly planted in the soil of Europe, and the second in that of America and Africa, so may the third Christian millennium witness a great harvest of faith on this vast and vital continent.'

Interestingly, President Vladimir Putin has met Pope Francis three times in the last eight years, but not once extended an invitation to him to visit Russia. The Russian Orthodox Church continues to hold on to the millennium-old stance of 'no welcome' for a papal visit. The orthodox denominations—in Russia and other countries—insist that the Catholics should desist from 'sheep-stealing', a euphemism for proselytizing. Interestingly, Catholics themselves complain about the same by the Mormons and Pentecostals in Europe and America.

These facts are important to understand a few basics. From Jawaharlal Nehru to Modi, all Indian PMs have upheld not only constitutional decorum but displayed the quintessential Indian ethos of respect for all religions. The Constitution of India zealously safeguards 'freedom of religion' as a fundamental right. It was in this spirit of pluralism that PM Modi met the Pope and invited him to India.

Christian missionaries of various denominations have made full use of this constitutional freedom and pluralist ethos to propagate their religion in India for centuries. There is no merit in the argument that Catholics do not convert. Catholic Christianity in India grew over centuries through the early proselytizing missions of the Portuguese and Spanish.

While there have been controversies over mass conversions and conversions through fraudulent means, the fundamental right of religious freedom has never been obstructed by any government in India, much less a BJP one. But then, if conversions are legitimate, so are reconversions, over which the apologists make a lot of hue and cry.

This victimhood politics has been integral to some missionaries and their apologists. 'Christianity in danger' is a red rag they liberally flaunt whenever they are asked to abide by the law of the land. The controversy over FCRA extension to Missionaries of Charity (MoC) is a case in point. Since then, several facts have come out. It was not just the MoC, thousands of other non-governmental organizations (NGOs) too were denied the extension on the grounds stipulated by the Ministry of Home Affairs (MHA). They included many Hindu charities and in one case, even a Seva Bharati affiliated NGO, which has connections with the Sangh Parivar. Many have appealed against the MHA's decision. In the MoC's case, the extension was granted despite their not going in for an appeal.

Yet the victimhood machine became hyperactive, from columns in the Indian media to calls in the British Parliament. No doubt, the ministry should have handled the matter more diligently. But the charity must also remember that it has an obligation to follow Indian law, which does not see religion in any applications. Many of them, including the MoC, are Christian NGOs. Diverting foreign funds for personal use like purchasing vehicles in personal names, distributing cash doles at weekly church gatherings and misusing them under administrative expenses invite scrutiny for which prestigious charities like the MoC must always be forthcoming. The bigger you are, the greater the scrutiny will be. A Nobel Prize does not exempt one from the law of the land.

Charity and service are not new to India, nor are they the exclusive domain of any religious institution. They are integral to Indian cultural life. The Sangh Parivar itself runs close to two lakh service projects in the remotest corners of the country. Missionaries run many educational and healthcare projects, as do Sikh, Jain, Buddhist and Muslim charities. But every time an act of charity or proselytism is scrutinized by law enforcement agencies, the apologists fling into action, casting communal motives on the government and castigating the Sangh Parivar. This is victimhood politics, pure and simple.

Sadly, it gains credibility when those on the other side resort to abusing even the good work that the missionaries do and glorifying controversies that surround such charities. Mother Teresa and her charity do attract some criticism globally, but so do many others of all religions. Linking the MHA's specific legal action to other controversies and casting aspersions on all missionary institutions will only perpetuate the myth that Christians are being persecuted in India.

40

The New Gender Agenda

Feminism in India should not fall victim to Western discourse. Dignity, freedom of choice and equity must be ensured for all women drawing inspiration from Indian ethos.

Women have been central to the civilizational discourse of many nations from ancient times. For Hindus, the creator-gods like Brahma, Vishnu and Shiva are incomplete without their female counterparts—Saraswati, Lakshmi and Shakti. The Western civilizations have their own female ancestors. It was Pandora for ancient Greeks and Eve for Judaeo-Christians. If the beauty of Helen was the cause of the Trojan War in ancient Greece, Hindus had their Sita and Draupadi at the root of the wars in the Ramayana and the Mahabharata.

However, the portrayal of womanhood in different traditions has been different. The stories of Pandora and Eve have greatly influenced Western traditions. Take the story of Pandora:

The Titan Prometheus was once assigned the task of creating the race of man. He afterwards grew displeased with the mean lot imposed on them by the gods and so stole fire from heaven. Zeus was angered and commanded Hephaistos and other gods to create the first woman Pandora, endowing her with beauty and cunningness. He then had her delivered to Prometheus' foolish younger brother Epimetheus as a bride.

Zeus gave Pandora a storage jar (pithos) as a wedding gift which she opened, releasing the swarm of evil spirits trapped within. These would forever after plague mankind.

This theme of a 'beautiful and cunning woman' continues in the story of the Trojan Wars in Homer's eight century BCE epic poems Iliad and Odyssey. Iliad was about a beautiful woman named Helen, queen of Sparta and wife of king Menelaus. She elopes with the Trojan prince Paris at the prodding of the capricious goddess Aphrodite. An enraged Menelaus dispatches his brother Agamemnon with a fleet of more than thousand ships to avenge the action of the Trojans. Agamemnon brings back Helen after killing Paris and destroying the city of Troy. All through the Homeric narrative, Helen comes across as a hapless and weak woman.

In the Judaeo-Christian tradition, the portrayal of Eve—the female companion of the first male, Adam, in the Book of Genesis—led to a profoundly negative impact on women in the West throughout the history of the last two millennia. Genesis in the Bible projects Eve as a quintessential evil, who disobeyed God. Eve's sin was to come under the evil spell of the serpent and encouraging Adam to eat the forbidden fruit in defiance of God's injunction. God punishes both for their disloyalty and expels them from the Garden of Eden. However, a greater punishment was reserved for Eve. 'I will greatly increase your pangs in childbearing; in pain you shall bring forth children; yet your desire shall be for your husband; and he shall rule over you,' God commanded.

Such narratives led to the Western women endure great discrimination and repressions at the hands of the religious establishment as well as in the lay Christian societies. They were not allowed to open their mouths in any assembly, not empowered at the pulpit and were generally treated as lesser humans. Thousands of women were branded as witches and put to brutal death in medieval Europe.

There was nobody to challenge the traditional repressive interpretations of the Genesis, hence, women themselves had to take up cudgels against it. That was how the Western feminist movement was born, which started challenging the misogynist and patriarchal interpretations of the Semitic religions. Renowned Australian feminist Geena D. Andersen puts it beautifully: 'Feminism is not about making women stronger. Women are already strong. It is about changing the way the world perceives their strength.'

Indian women did not face such challenges. Portrayal of their ancestors in Hindu tradition was one of courage, freedom and wisdom. Sita of Ramayana was a woman with self-dignity who refuses to return to Ram and instead chooses to go back to her mother, the Mother Earth. Draupadi in Mahabharata was a feisty and ferocious woman who refuses to accede to anything short of the blood of Dushasana even if that meant an epic war. Maitreyi engages in a scholarly debate with her husband Sage Yajnavalkya on the issue of the omnipresent and relents only when the sage warns that she had reached the question of the questions beyond which no more questions exist. After declaring her husband Mandana Misra, a loser in a debate with Adi Shankara, Ubhaya Bharati challenges Shankara to debate with her on Kama Vidya—the science of sexuality, forcing him to retreat for a duration and return with that knowledge. Chivalrous Rani Lakshmibai of Jhansi and philosopher queen Ahilya Bai Holkar of Indore led armies from the front against the British. In James Mill's *The History of British India*, Prof. H.H. Wilson says: 'It may be confidently asserted that in no nation of antiquity were women held in so much esteem as amongst Hindus.'

But the contemporary Indian society has drifted away from those ideals in its treatment of women. Pendulum swings between objectification and over-restriction for Indian women today. Contemporary moralism in India was a Victorian-era import, which was rejected as anti-women by the colonists themselves. Security of women became a very patronizing chauvinism leading to denial of choice to them. Dignity, freedom of choice and equity, the traditional values of Indian ethos, thus elude Indian women today. The result is that while India ranks eighteenth in the world in terms of political empowerment of women, thereby placing it ahead of many other countries including 'developed' ones, it tragically ranks 150th in women's health and survival, 112th in education attainment and 149th in economic participation and opportunity.[39]

How would it change? In a letter written to Rajkumari Amrit Kaur in October 1936, Gandhi, a Sanatani Hindu, had this advice for the women of India:

> If you women only realise your dignity and privilege, and make full sense of it for mankind, you will make it much better than it is. But man has delighted in enslaving you and you have proved willing slaves till the slave and holders have become one in the crime of degrading humanity. My special function from childhood, you might say, has been to make women realise their dignity. I was once a slave holder myself but Ba (Kasturba) proved an unwilling slave and thus opened my eyes to my mission.

Gandhi's call was for women to take up cudgels like their Western counterparts to ameliorate this situation. But while doing so, they shouldn't fall victim to the Western discourse. Women issues in India should be placed and reviewed in

---

[39]'Global Gender Gap Report 2020', *World Economic Forum*, 2019, http://tinyurl.com/ym34f23t. Accessed on 12 January 2024.

the Indian context. Terms like 'equality' and 'empowerment' betray only a partial challenge in the Indian context. If empowerment means a tokenism like women securing some positions, political or otherwise, India is probably performing better than others. Do those words merely mean that an equal number of women should occupy positions as that of men while all other women remain in a choice-less patriarchy? Or the real issue is about dignity, freedom of choice and equity irrespective of empowerment? Amanda Gorman, the young Black American girl who recited at Biden's inauguration, has said that her opportunity doesn't reflect the general condition of the Black American women. India's women's movement needs to revisit these issues through a purely Indian lens.

Reprinted from CHINTAN–INDIA FOUNDATION BLOGS, with permission of India Foundation.

41

Overcoming the Partition of the Minds

Three major partitions happened in the world in the second half of the 1940s. Germany was partitioned into the Eastern and Western blocs in 1945, followed by India into Hindustan and Pakistan in 1947. Finally, Israel was created by partitioning Palestine in 1948.

Germany's partition was temporary. The Berlin Wall, constructed in the early 1960s to accord permanence to it, was dismantled by the Germans in less than three decades. The country was reunified in 1989.

But in India and Palestine, partition was a terrible affair, leading to a full-scale war in Israel and mass migration accompanied by mind-numbing violence in India.

The Arab-Israel war at the time of the partition of Palestine in 1947–49 caused the death of over 30,000 people. But the death and destruction caused at the time of India's Partition were horrifying.

More than a million were murdered, while many more had to endure a treacherous migration across the hastily created border, often on foot. Hundreds of thousands could not make it, as they were waylaid and butchered.

Those horrors are difficult to forget. Historian William Dalrymple, in an article in *New Yorker*, quotes from a book by Nisid Hajari, *Midnight's Furies: The Deadly Legacy of India's*

Partition, about the brutality of the period:

> Gangs of killers set whole villages aflame, hacking to death men and children and the aged while carrying off young women to be raped. Some British soldiers and journalists who witnessed the Nazi death camps claimed Partition's brutalities were worse: pregnant women had their breasts cut off and babies hacked out of their bellies; infants were found literally roasted on spits.

Partition of India was a meaningless and reckless act. Mahatma Gandhi opposed it saying: 'Vivisect me before vivisecting India'. Sardar Vallabhbhai Patel vowed to fight till the end to reject it. Rajendra Prasad conclusively proved its irrationality in a thoroughly argued 1946-book, *India Divided*.

Across the border, for Saadat Hasan Manto, the famed author, it was all sheer madness. Those women raped, with bulged stomachs, distressed him. 'Where should those bellies belong to—Hindustan or Pakistan?' Manto questioned in innocent grief. His dark satire on Partition-time madness, 'Toba Tek Singh', ends with his eponymous hero Tek Singh seen stranded on no-man's land between the newly created India and Pakistan. 'On one side, behind barbed wire, stood together the lunatics of India and on the other side, behind more barbed wire, stood the lunatics of Pakistan. In between, on a bit of earth which had no name, lay Toba Tek Singh,' Manto provocatively demurs.

Partition was not inevitable even until the early 1940s. But then, the British were in a hurry to leave. Louis Mountbatten arrived in India in March 1947 with the mandate to free the country before June 1948. After meeting Muhammad Ali Jinnah, 'a psychopathic case', Mountbatten decided not to wait for that long. In June, he unilaterally declared that the British would partition India and leave in less than three months.

Gandhi could not reconcile to the fact that a 'maniac' and 'an evil genius' like Jinnah could have his way, and retreated to Bengal to attend to the victims of the bigotry and brutality of its rabid communalist premier, Huseyn Suhrawardy. Jawaharlal Nehru, who once called Partition 'fantastic nonsense', reconciled quickly and declared in April 1947, 'I want that those who stand as an obstacle in our way should go their own way.'

In India, Rajendra Prasad became the first president of partitioned India, and Nehru its first Prime Minister (PM). In Pakistan, Manto was branded a traitor and thrown into jail, and he died a broken man in 1955 at the age of 42.

For Hindus, Partition was not merely a loss of territory; it was the vivisection of their revered motherland. The urge for undoing it and reclaiming that lost territory, Akhand Bharat, remains a fervent dream for many of them, as Israel remained for the Jews for over two millennia.

The partition of Germany was rejected by people on both sides of the Berlin Wall. They pulled it down and ended the colonial game. Both, the last PM of East Germany, Lothar de Maizière, and the leader of Opposition, Richard Schröder, stood by their people. Despite domestic opposition in the Soviet Union, Mikhail Gorbachev demonstrated statesmanship by not interfering.

Unfortunately, the Partition of India was not just about land, but about minds. The premise was that Hindus and Muslims cannot live together. Jinnah, who was once hailed as 'the Ambassador of Hindu-Muslim Unity' and had disparagingly dismissed the propaganda about Hindu domination as just 'a bogey, put before you [Muslims] by your enemies to frighten you', turned the tables by the 1940s and maniacally argued that they could never live together. He won.

The first step to Akhand Bharat would be to bottle the Jinnah genie. Partition-time memories should help mitigate the wounds that communities nurture and end the mental and emotional divide, not exacerbate it further. 'This day will not only inspire us to eliminate the poison of discrimination, animosity and ill will, but it will also strengthen unity, social harmony and human sensibilities,' PM Narendra Modi fervently hoped when he recently called for the Partition Horrors Remembrance Day to be observed every 14 August. May the day be marked with this spirit.

42

Neoliberals and Their Shenanigans

Liberalism of the Enlightenment era thinkers like John Locke and Adam Smith was about political and economic liberty. Individual freedom, human rights, minimalist state, democracy and economic liberty were its desideratum.

Franklin Delano Roosevelt had added welfarism to it after World War II and projected it as the progressive liberalism or simply the progressivism.

The Second Bill of Rights that Roosevelt talked about in his State of the Union address in 1944 was about 'a useful and remunerative job', 'a decent home' and 'a good education' to the citizens.

There is another kind of welfarism pioneered by Bismarck in the united Germany in the nineteenth century. It was liberalism without liberty. He created an authoritarian state while keeping people happy with trinkets.

Marx had described it as 'democracy in substance' as against the 'democracy by election' of the West.

The leitmotif of the Chinese Communist state is the liberalism of Bismarck or the Prussians, in which 'alleviation of material and educational poverty, and liberation from old dogmas and old faiths' were considered the substance.

'China is a country more focused on the welfare of

the totality of its people, and these government actions are considered acceptable paths to alleviating poverty and ensuring shared prosperity,' the official Chinese media claims.

Chinese leaders admonish their American counterparts for raking up issues like Xinxiang and Tibet or the authoritative control of the Communist Party of China insisting that their system is based on 'Asian values'.

Progressive Liberalism has been the mainstay of the sociopolitical value system of many countries including India for centuries. The Constitution of India has also been founded on those principles.

There was just one bizarre exception during Emergency in 1975–77, but largely the Indian political system has always stood for democratic freedoms and economic welfarism in the last more than seven decades.

Incidentally, liberalism has not stopped with progressivism. A neoliberal creed has emerged in the West in the last few decades. It is a negationist creed based on identity politics.

Once champions of universalism and critics of identity politics of the conservatives, the neoliberals have reduced all the classical and progressive liberalist ideals to identity politics of racial minorities, queer groups and imagined communities.

Those causes per se may not be unworthy. But the problem with the neoliberals is their propensity to use identity causes like same sex marriages, live-in relations and minorityism as political weapons to challenge the establishments ignoring larger cultural and social consequences.

Their war is not against the conservatives alone, it is against the progressive liberals too. In their ebullience, the neoliberals do not mind siding with dictators and supporting violence.

Many liberals believed that the Soviet Union was the freest place on earth. John Dewey, a renowned American liberal scholar of the last century, had authored a series of articles on the Soviet Union for the *The New Republic*, gloating smugly that it was a grand 'experiment' for the 'liberation of a people to consciousness of themselves as a determining power in the shaping of their ultimate fate'. Today, a section of them want the American leadership to see virtues in China.

'The consequences of not getting the Chinese challenge right today will be vaster still. A cold war with China is likely to be much longer and more costly than the one with the Soviet Union, with an uncertain outcome,' warned liberal commentator Fareed Zakaria in *Foreign Affairs* magazine.

When race riots broke out on the West Coast city of Watts, there stood American liberal elites unapologetically supporting the rioters. They blamed White America—'the system'—for the violence, and provided a morally admirable name for it—'rebellion'.

Hubert Humphrey, the liberal vice-president of America, lamented that if he'd been born poor, he too might have rioted. An entire 'riot ideology' was discovered, and the liberals use that to justify the race riots in America and the Delhi riots in India.

These neoliberal shenanigans have arrived in India long ago, in universities and academic and intellectual hotspots. They champion all destructive causes and insist that they should pass off as fundamental freedoms.

When challenged, they blame the 'system', calling it 'revisionist', 'fascist' and 'Hindu nationalist'. While spitting out volumes of calumny against the government on a daily basis, they still shout from the rooftops that there was no 'freedom of expression'. If action is taken against wrongdoers, they immediately google for their caste, religion and community to badger the government for being 'illiberal'. One journalist's arrest for wrongdoing becomes 'an assault on entire free press'.

When the judiciary follows Constitutional procedures, it gets branded as 'compromised'.

The agencies become 'agents' for performing their duties. There are not many takers for these neoliberals in India, but they have amplifiers in international liberalsphere aplenty.

The liberalsphere has the potential to damage the reputation globally. Recent Freedom House's report lowering India's ranking from 71[40] to 67[41], is a case in point. By their relentless campaign, the neoliberals have succeeded in creating an impression that freedom is at risk in India.

A careful scrutiny of the report indicates that it is largely based on heresy and hypotheses. India was ranked 71st in the last report and was in the category of a 'free' country. It dropped by 4 points and became 'partly free' now.

Its score dropped in four areas—judiciary, pandemic-time harsh lockdown measures, restrictions on foreign funding of the non government organisations (NGOs) and sedition and other charges against free speech.

The Freedom House believes that Indian judiciary is compromised because the Supreme Court has given a few judgements favourable to the government. It says that the lockdown during the Covid-19 pandemic was harsh and caused suffering to poor citizens like migrants.

There can't be more frivolous arguments than these. Equally ludicrous are the exaggerated insinuations that the NGO sector is being harassed or 'dozens of journalists' have been incarcerated under sedition laws.

The suggestion that journalists have been co-opted by the government is a serious charge against the Indian media,

---

[40]'Freedom in the World 2020', *Freedom House*, http://tinyurl.com/y27exfv2. Accessed on 29 January 2024.

[41]'Freedom in the World 2021', *Freedom House*, http://tinyurl.com/3t9jz8ze. Accessed on 29 January 2024.

which has to respond to Freedom House slander.

However, self-righteous indignation is not enough to handle such liberal caterwauling. Irrespective of what we say in Parliament and outside, we care for the image of the leader and the government.

Hence, respond to the 'sermons' with facts and arguments. The ranking of America has dropped from a past high of 94 to 83 this year. Yang Jiechi, the Chinese Special Representative, has used last year's race riots to attack America at the Alaska meeting. US Secretary of State Antony Blinken's response is instructive. '(The US was engaged in a) constant quest to form a more perfect union and that quest acknowledges our imperfections,' he said with dignity.

Reprinted from SWARAJYA, with permission of Kovai Media Pvt. Ltd.

43

Why Big Tech Needs Regulation

'You will leave the relevance of the questions to me,' Minister for Home Affairs K. Shanmugam curtly told Facebook officials when they objected to his questions in an official inquiry commission. 'You do not want to be regulated. (But) We look at your conduct all over the world. We are looking at our national security,' Shanmugam told the officials to their face, and refused to engage further by saying, 'Can we move on? I don't need an answer from you.' What followed were stringent laws regulating social media in the case of fake news and other libelous posts.

Australians, too, took a tough line in dealing with Facebook and Google. Scott Morrison, ex-prime minister of Australia, had faced stiff resistance from Facebook when he proposed revenue sharing for news with local media houses. Both Facebook and Google went on the offensive against the move and even resorted to a news blackout including news about emergency services. Seventy per cent of Australia's population uses Facebook. But Morrison did not budge. With the support of the opposition Labor Party, he got the Bill passed in Australian Parliament. He even tried to elicit global support for his endeavour to stand up to the big tech. 'They may be changing the world, but that doesn't mean they should run it. We will not be intimidated by this act of bullying by Big Tech,' Morrison bluntly said.

Big tech companies, including social media giants, have grown big and powerful. With size, grew their indifference and intransigence too. Governments are increasingly finding it untenable. Countries like China, Russia and North Korea used their authoritarian regimes to take a hard line against the tech giants. Several European countries have taken steps to limit the power of these big tech companies and protect the privacy of their citizens. Having experienced the unprecedented power of these companies including the audacity to ban the X (formerly Twitter) handle of the president of the country, the US has initiated hearings to look into the possible power abuse committed by Google, Facebook and Amazon.

In comparison, the Government of India's response can be described as mild and moderate. X should understand this from the fact that instead of dismissing its self-righteous statement accusing the Indian police of 'use of intimidation tactics' and a 'potential threat to freedom of expression for the people we serve', the IT Ministry thought it necessary to issue a lengthy three-page rebuttal.

X was certainly wrong in branding tweets highlighting the alleged Congress toolkit as 'manipulative media' when an investigation by police was underway. A mere complaint by the accused, the Congress party, should not have been used by X to resort to tagging the tweets of senior Bharatiya Janata Party (BJP) leaders as 'manipulative media'. If X had any evidence of manipulation, it was duty-bound to share the same with the police. The police went to X's office seeking just that. Instead, X chose to play the victim card.

We are living in a technology-intensive world. The twenty-first century world has moved on from multipolarity to 'heteropolarity'. A heteropolitan world is one in which international power is no longer limited to national governments. It is geographically dispersed and led by many different players with divergent objectives challenging the authority of national governments. These players include multinational tech giants such as Facebook, Google and X, global non-governmental organization (NGO), transnational terror groups like ISIS and religious organizations.

Heteropolitan players pose new challenges to nations. The last time that India faced such a challenge was when Disha Ravi and Greta Thunberg used another toolkit to exploit the farmers' agitation and spread discord and dissonance about the Indian government globally. In the absence of any regulatory laws for social media, the Indian state was forced to resort to existing laws such as Unlawful Activities (Prevention) Act (UAPA) and sedition. Champions of free speech had vociferously condemned the slapping of sedition laws against Disha Ravi and Greta then. It is true that the national laws of many countries were inadequate in dealing with these new challenges. The new situation demanded new legislation. India took its time to come up with legislation in this regard recently. The tech giants must realize that it is a better situation than using British-era archaic laws such as sedition or anti-terrorism laws such as UAPA.

While the new situation compelled national governments to promulgate new laws to tackle fake news and other online offenses, it also must be remembered that the means of communication have been universalized and democratized by social media platforms. The primary way of tackling this situation should be through better communication. There is also a need for enhanced levels of tolerance to dissent. Digital and social media are democratic in nature. Hence, while trying to regulate them through legislation, extreme judiciousness is required to ensure that the broader democratic ethos is not compromised.

At the same time, the expectation that online campaigns

that spread discord and dissonance must be tolerated in the name of free speech or because of the age, gender and food habits of the activists, as witnessed during the trial of Disha Ravi, is an unacceptable proposition. Social media platforms cannot fully escape the blame of political bias. Complaints of deliberate bias abound about the behaviour of certain social media companies in India and elsewhere.

We are passing through a transition into the heteropolar world. There will be debates over actions of the governments. Tech giants controlling social media platforms stubbornly resist any regulatory efforts by the governments. It is important to build a national consensus over the need for a rational regulation that would not affect free speech but help protect the privacy and dignity of the individuals.

Big tech companies such as Google, Facebook and X cannot continue to resist these moves claiming self-regulation. Emmanuel Macron, the French President, had told them, while proposing measures against fake news in his country, that in order for the internet to be truly 'free, open and secure', some sort of a regulation 'is the sine qua non condition'.

Courtesy: India Today Digital.

44

Democracy and Social Media

Technological innovations are not going to stop. But those responsible for those innovations must remember that it was democratic freedom and human rights that have helped their innovations flourish. They should ensure that those values survive and grow.

As Benjamin Franklin, one of the founding fathers of the American constitution, walked out of the famed Independence Hall, where he and another 54 delegates from all over USA had gathered from 25 May to 17 September 1787 to prepare the American constitution, he was asked what type of government the delegates had decided to create. 'A republic, if you can keep it,' he had famously replied. It was a profound statement suggesting that they didn't just create another form of government—the republic, where people rule themselves through their elected representatives—but a precious one, which requires eternal vigilance and timely action to keep.

The democratic republics have faced many challenges in the last couple of centuries. They witnessed elections throwing up demagogues and dictators. They saw democracies turning into mobocracies. The republics weathered those challenges and not only survived but flourished. By the end of the last century, the world became more democratic than before, with more than a hundred countries worldwide embracing the democratic republican model for governance. Democracies were touted as the panacea for the mankind. The American leadership has built a strategic doctrine around making the world more democratic. India opted for it after Independence and emerged as a successful democracy some seven decades ago. America, as the oldest and India as the largest democracy, stood as beacons of hope for the freedom-loving humanity.

However, signs of a new tumult are increasingly becoming discernible in the last couple of decades. Technological innovations in areas like information technology (IT) have started to transform political landscapes also. Initially, the IT revolution had helped in empowering democracies. When people of the erstwhile Soviet republics wanted to unshackle themselves from Communist dictatorship, they found fax machines as a useful weapon. Audio and video cassettes became handy for political mobilization, subsequently. By the end of the century, the World Wide Web has completely revolutionized the political communication landscape. The gang-rape of a teenage, Oksana Makar in Ukraine, had led to a major revolt against the powerful ruling lobby led by President Yanukovych simply because the victim's mother chose to upload the gory video of her daughter in coma after the rape on to the web.

Then came the Arab Spring in 2010, which continued for three years and engulfed 17–18 Arab countries like a wildfire. It all began in Tunisia when a petty merchant named Mohammed Bouazizi refused to bribe police officers and instead committed self-immolation in broad public view. Bouazizi's bold defiance of Tunisia's authoritarian and corrupt leadership was captured live and transmitted through social media platforms like X and Facebook. Soon began what some analysts described as the 'Twitter Revolution' in more than a dozen Arab countries, including Libya, Egypt and Syria. A study conducted by the Dubai School of Government titled the Arab Social Media Report analysed social media's impact in the Arab Spring.

It concluded that 'the growth of social media in the region and the shift in usage trends have played a critical role in mobilisation, empowerment, shaping opinions, and influencing change.' The report had also stated that almost 85 per cent of Egyptians and 86 per cent of Tunisians admitted to using social media to 'spread awareness, spread information, or organise actions'.[42] India too experienced its own versions of social media-driven revolution like the one led by Anna Hazare.

Suddenly, it dawned on the political elite that the new technological revolution of the new century has not only given certain powerful social media tools to empower citizens but transform them into formidable weapons. They are posing a new challenge to humanity about which Albert Einstein had warned decades ago. Technological advances 'could have made human life carefree and happy if the development of the organising power of man had been able to keep step with his technical advances,' he warned suggesting that failure to 'keep step' would be 'as dangerous as a razor in the hands of a three-year-old child'.

Technology, along with globalization and economic trends, has made 'power easier to get, but harder to use or keep', wrote Venezuelan Journalist Moisés Naím in his book, *The End of Power*, highlighting the present dilemma. The new media has taught people how to disrupt, while a clear formula to bridge the gap between disruption and legitimacy still eludes. The digital era that unfolded as a great promise stands out today as the greatest challenge for democracies. A tussle is breaking out between the authoritarian regimes that want to control and eavesdrop on the digital data to monitor their own

---

[42]Arab Social Media Report, *Civil Movements: The Impact of Facebook and Twitter,* May 2011, http://tinyurl.com/mu2ny4a7. Accessed on 25 January 2024.

populations and equally belligerent and anarchist user groups that want to weaponize it for creating large scale disruption and disharmony in the system. The victim, either way, is the traditional democratic value system that we so fondly cherished in all these decades.

Who is accountable? The authoritarians or the anarchists or the digital platforms like Facebook and X? Leaders, like K. Shanmugam, the minister of law of Singapore, to Emmanuel Macron, the French president to many more, are struggling to find answers to these questions. Jacinda Ardern, former prime minister (PM) of New Zealand, wanted social media platforms like Facebook to be made accountable, insisting that 'it cannot be the case of all profits and no responsibility'. While proposing measures against fake news in his country, Macron argued that in order for the internet to be truly 'free, open and secure', some sort of a regulation 'is the sine qua non condition'.

But the platforms do not seem willing to accept accountability to democratic societies. The 17 million Australian users of Facebook have tasted its fury when it blocked out entire news, including some emergency services on its platform, as a retaliation to the Australian Parliament's bid to bind the global technology giant to a certain geography and the law of the land. Scott Morrison, the former Australian PM has secured the support of the opposition Labour Party in the Parliament. He also reached out to a number of world leaders, including PM Narendra Modi, to bolster support for his bold move. 'They may be changing the world, but that doesn't mean they should run it,' Morrison argued, perhaps rightly.

After its repeated efforts to encourage social media giants to self-regulate failed, the Singapore government has come out with a stringent Protection from Online Falsehoods and Manipulation Act (POFMA) in 2019. The Minister of Law

K. Shanmugam dismissed protestations from the platforms and said that the law was necessary because the platforms that often host fake news have business models that depend on 'attracting eyeballs'. 'The tendency has been on the side of the internet platforms to say: hey, it's free speech, there shouldn't be any regulation of it. Let's be frank when social media platforms argue against it (regulation), it's really putting profit above principle,' Shanmugam, who is also Singapore's home minister, said bluntly.

The Government of India, too, appears to be bracing for a collision with these digital titans by trying to regulate them. Like several other democracies, it too lacked a proper legal framework to tackle the new digital challenge posed by these titans that refuse to recognize geographical boundaries and national laws.

Denmark has attempted something unique. It appointed one of its senior and respected diplomats, Casper Klynge as the first-ever ambassador to Silicon Valley, with a mandate to engage with technology giants like Amazon, Facebook and Google. Klynge has been trying to popularize the term 'techplomacy'. Denmark's goal was to place ambassadors at 'epicentres of transformation around the world' to better understand the impact of technology on Danish society and how to prepare for an increasingly digital world, Klynge explains.

Seven decades ago, in August 1949, a significantly improved Geneva Convention was adopted to secure the fundamental rights of the soldiers and civilians during times of war. Dominic Carr of Microsoft proposed that it is time 'for a Digital Geneva Convention', which would help protect citizens on the internet during the time of peace. Techplomacy and Digital Geneva Convention are the best way forward to ensure judicious regulation of the new technologies of communication.

Technological innovations are not going to stop. But those responsible for those innovations must remember that it was democratic freedom and human rights that have helped their innovations flourish. They should ensure that those values survive and flourish. As Einstein pointed out, technological innovations call for speeding up of the work to manage them too.

Reprinted from ORGANISER, with permission of Bharat Prakashan (Delhi) Limited.

45

Gandhi's True Legacy

On 30 January 1948, the flag of the United Nations was lowered to half-mast. For the first time, the United Nations had set aside a day's session to honour the man just murdered in Delhi. 'Not the head of a state, a general or a king, but a lone man who without an army, riches, or political alliances, has been called the most powerful man of the 20th century. Who was this man that all the world should mourn over?'—Encyclopedia Britannica's documentary on Gandhi begins with this description. Gandhi's greatness is universal. For Gandhians, he is an eternal inspiration. Gandhi never hated anybody, but some Gandhians do. Incidentally, for those whom Gandhians hate, too, Gandhi is iconic, for Gandhi fits into all shapes and sizes. His legacy can be appropriated by anyone. As is famously said of leaders, Gandhi too can be 'loved or hated but not ignored'.

Gandhi had optimistically predicted that he could be killed but not his Gandhism. Seventy-two years after his death, Gandhism remains, but it is largely about externals. Cleanliness, khadi, cow protection and swadeshi became chic in Gandhi's name. Gandhi emerged as a 'trendy fashion icon'. These are not unimportant. But Gandhism is much more than these externals.

Gandhi's core message was about freedom, which Tagore described in his poem as 'where the mind is without fear'.

Enlightenment thinkers emphasized on human freedom from the material standpoint. Gandhi gave this a spiritual dimension. From South Africa to India, Gandhi relentlessly fought for freedom and equality. He aligned freedom with responsibility and equality with dignity and love. 'I am not interested in freeing India from merely English yoke. I am bent on freeing India from any yoke whatsoever,' Gandhi declared. Biographer Louis Fischer quipped that the Englishman who pushed Gandhi out of the railway carriage in South Africa didn't realize that in a few decades, the same fragile man would push the English Raj out of India.

Nat Turner, the African American slave-preacher, too, was born on 2 October in 1800. Turner was the first to rebel against slavery in America. His rebellion was crushed and he was hanged. Like Gandhi, Turner too trod the spiritual path like a mystic. He too was austere in his lifestyle and fasted and prayed regularly. Like Gandhi, he also believed that his mission was divine.

Gandhi carried forward Turner's mantle in South Africa, fighting against apartheid. Later, in India, he led the struggle against the British rule on the one hand and social evils on the other. He described the movement for *swaraj* as one of 'self-purification'.

Gandhism lies in the commitment to freedom and self-purification. Dictators thrive on yokes like brute state power, a pliant media and incessant propaganda. Gandhi respected his critics. But dictators can't stand dissent. They live in their cocoons, surrounded by henchmen and yes-men. That has been the story, from Hitler to Stalin. Once the Third Reich was formed in 1933, Hitler declared that the party had no more role in the government. He surrounded himself with 'experts'. Leaders who came before him were erased from the historic memory. Stalin undertook the 'Great Purge', eliminating his competitors and rivals in the party starting with the killing of Sergei Kirov in 1934 and ending with the killing of Leon Trotsky in 1940. In all these campaigns, both Hitler and Stalin depended on state power and a submissive media.

Gandhi was the antithesis of such dictatorial tendencies. Gandhi lived an open life, never surrounded by a coterie. He was fearless in truth. He rushed to Noakhali when riots broke out in early 1947 in which a large number of Hindus were killed. For four months, he went from village to village persuading Muslims to embrace their Hindu neighbours. He admonished Huseyn Suhrawardy, the Bengal Premier, for his inaction. But then, he refused to accept the chief minister's version about the communal situation in Bihar and rushed to Patna to offer succour to Muslims who were victimized by Hindus. He admonished the Congress government in equally harsh words for its failure.

That's what Gandhi called Ram Rajya or Dharma Rajya—a state of righteous freedom. Deendayal Upadhyaya later explained Dharma Rajya in the terms of democracy. Democracy is understood as the government 'by the people, of the people and for the people'. According to Deendayal, while 'by the people' and 'of the people' represented elections and government, 'for the people' meant Dharma Rajya. Ram Rajya, for Gandhi, meant people being free from every type of yoke.

Gandhi's saga inspired many. Authoritarian regimes fell in many countries after India. The last to fall in the last century was the Soviet Union. The Soviet regime's anthem used to describe the country as the 'indestructible union of free republics'. Those republics were barely free under the Soviet regime. The myth of indestructibility remained only until Mikhail Gorbachev became the president in 1986. All that was needed for the indestructibility to go was his policy of Glasnost—openness. The Kazakhs were the first to take to the streets in 1986. Gorbachev used brute military power, but the movement for freedom spread like a wildfire, destroying one of the last surviving dictatorships of the twentieth century. Horrific details of the accident at the Chernobyl nuclear power plant were carried by the recently 'freed' Russian media far and wide, further precipitating the downfall.

There is a growing democracy deficit in the world today. People's freedoms are at stake. The Gandhian agenda was always about more openness, freedom and a life of dignity and respect. A benevolent state and a free media are mandatory for people's freedom. 'I will be gone saying what I am saying, but one-day people will remember that what this poor man said, that alone was true,' Gandhi pleaded once. Realizing that Gandhi was right is real Gandhism.

46

The Soul of the Nation

India differs from the West in the ethical foundations of its nationalism and its idea of the state. Nationalism is the new flavour of the season in the world. Many scholars predict that the post-pandemic world order will witness a further rise of nationalism in many countries. The healthcare challenge posed by the pandemic has led to countries turning inwards. The much-touted globalization and unipolarity seem passé now.

The nationalism that Western scholars are talking about was a much-loathed idea until recently. It was associated with dictators like Hitler and Mussolini and dismissed as chauvinistic and dangerous. Liberal globalism and constitutional moralism were touted as the new order. Yet, in less than eight decades after the dreadful World War II in which over 80 million[43] deaths and extensive destruction and displacement occurred, nationalist forces are back in many countries. Unfortunately, the return of nationalism on the world stage need not be good news. Today's nationalism in the West is a response to certain contemporary challenges like illegal immigration, racial rivalries and the collapse of globalization and multiculturalism. The pandemic has added urgency to it.

The nationalism discourse is a recent phenomenon in the West. It started with the rise of nation states in Europe a

[43]'World War II Casualties by Country 2024', *World Population Review*, http://tinyurl.com/2d839phb. Accessed on 9 January 2024.

couple of centuries ago. Nation states came into existence after the Reformation in the sixteenth and seventeenth centuries in Europe, when countries started untangling from the control of religious authorities. From that time Libya was invaded by Italy in 1911, setting off a chain of events leading to World War I, nationalism was seen as a panacea for mankind. Jefferson's United States of America, Napoleon's France, Bismarck's Germany and the United Kingdom were all hailed as the sentinels of nationalism.

'The concept of nation-states, that the aspirations of the people that constitute a nation are best served by a common political entity, is considered a relatively recent idea in Europe from the 18th century. Nationalism led to the formation of nation-states and modern countries,' wrote author Sankrant Sanu in an enlightening article, 'Why India Is a Nation'.[44]

British history of the last 200 years is a case in point. England, Scotland and Wales got together in 1707 in what was called the Great Britain. Even after coming together, they had retained different laws and held on to separate national churches. Scotland had an old Presbyterian Church order. It is in a way the national Church of Scotland and is known as Kirk. The English continue to have Anglican Christianity as their state religion. Although an Anglican Church, the Church of Wales has its own archbishop who is independent of the Anglican establishment of England.

Great Britain became the United Kingdom of Great Britain and Ireland when it annexed Ireland in 1801 using political, military and religious power. However, the Catholic majority in Ireland never accepted this arrangement and a long, bloody struggle followed, which culminated in the Catholic

---

[44]'Why India Is A Nation', *Sankrant.org*, 9 October 2003, http://tinyurl.com/4xxxxfb5. Accessed on 22 January 2024.

areas of southern Ireland seceding in 1922 to emerge again as the Republic of Ireland. By that time, the Anglican Church had ensured that its followers become a dominant group in Northern Ireland and continued their allegiance to the UK. Northern Ireland remained a part of the UK. Thus, the state of the UK that we see today can boast not even of a century's history.

American history, too, tells the same story. At the beginning of the eighteenth century, the Anglo-Saxon voyagers, who had sailed to the shores of the eastern coast of America and anchored near Boston, were hardly in control of less than 10 per cent of the geographical entity of what is today the US. At the time of the American Revolution in 1776, when the 13 British colonies came together and declared independence from the control of the British parliament, their geographical area was limited to the area covering the states on today's East Coast. Texas and California joined the union in 1845 after the Mexican war and Hawaii became a state in 1900. Seen from this historical background, the US as a nation state is not more than two centuries old.

Has the US emerged as a nation yet? This is a raging debate among academics in the West even now. The Second Continental Congress had declared American independence in July 1776 and adopted the United States Declaration of Independence drafted by Thomas Jefferson. In 1788, the new American constitution was adopted. The Bill of Rights, the most important first ten Articles of the US constitution, was adopted in 1791. It is this Bill of Rights that keep the diverse American people together.

In his important work, *Who Are We?: The Challenges to America's National Identity*, Samuel Huntington raised the crucial question as to whether it was enough. He writes:

> Globalisation, multiculturalism, cosmopolitanism, immigration, sub-nationalism, and anti-nationalism had battered American consciousness. Ethnic, gender and racial identities came to the fore. In contrast to their predecessors, many immigrants were ampersands, maintaining dual loyalties, and dual citizenships. A massive Hispanic influx raised questions concerning America's linguistic and cultural unity. Corporate executives, professionals and Information Age technocrats espoused cosmopolitan over national identities. The teaching of national history gave way to the teaching of ethnic and racial histories. The celebration of diversity replaced emphasis on what Americans had in common. The national unity and the sense of national identity created by work and war in the eighteenth and nineteenth centuries and consolidated in the world wars of the twentieth century seemed to be eroding. By 2000, America was, in many respects, less a nation than it had been for a century. The Stars and Stripes were at half-mast and other flags flew higher on the flagpole of American identities.

The nation states in Africa were a creation of the colonists. During 1884–85, European nations had held a meeting called the West Africa Conference in Berlin to discuss the partitioning of Africa. In a series of treaties in 1890–91, colonial boundaries were completely redrawn. What is most important to note is that not a single representative of the African people was involved when the colonial masters were redrawing the boundaries and creating the nation states in Africa.

There are a few countries in the world that can claim much longer history. For example, countries in South America like Mexico and countries in Eurasia like Egypt and Turkey, to name a few. But here again the nation states of all these countries are of very recent origin and had nothing to do with their ancient civilizational past. The ancient Mayan culture that was predominant in Mexico or the Aztec culture of the medieval period have largely remained today as museum pieces while the present-day Mexican society has become Hispanic in language, religion and culture. The case is the same with countries like Egypt and Turkey. The ancient kingdoms of Mesopotamia, Egypt, etc., had lost all their traces in the modern nation states of Egypt, Italy and Turkey.

All this points to the fact that the global understanding of the concept of nation and nationhood is based on short-lived models shifting their bases constantly. Yet, based on this short experience of last two centuries, various scholars in the West attempted to develop theories for nation and nationalism. Ethnicity, language, kinship, culture, territory and several other factors have been enumerated by these scholars as the basis for nationalism.

The Church's and Rome's political dominance was challenged by the Reformation. The Reformists had vehemently argued that there was no need for the Church to reach heaven, and thus the road to wisdom and heaven need not pass through Rome. In his illuminating article, legal luminary and Biblical scholar Lynn Buzzard wrote, 'The Protestant Reformation helped shatter the religious unity of Europe, and it was linked with the emergence of nation-states with their own boundaries, legislatures, jurisdiction, and therefore laws. It was a time of growing national consciousness. In place of the authority of Rome or the papacy or some universal principle, the source of the law's authority now became the state.'[45]

Many Western scholars consider the Peace of Westphalia

[45]Buzzard, Lynn, 'Stop! In the Name of the Law', *World*, 31 July 1999, http://tinyurl.com/m86ccfat. Accessed on 12 January 2024.

of 1648, which brought the bloody Thirty Years' War between the Catholics and the Protestants in Europe to an end, as the birth date of the nation state. The Peace of Westphalia had made the kings and rulers the sovereign authority over their respective territories, replacing the Catholic Church's authority.

European nationalism was a product of wars and conflicts. They needed the 'other' to define and fortify their national identities. Wars with France had brought the English, the Welsh and the Scots together to form a 'Protestant nation' called the Great Britain against the 'Catholic' aggressions. In his work *War and the Nation State*, historian Michael Howard argued, 'No nation, in the true sense of the word, could be born without war…no self-conscious community could establish itself as a new and independent actor on the world scene without an armed conflict or the threat of one.'

Despite definitional worries, there was some agreement among Western scholars about the most typical, paradigmatic form of nationalism. Territorial sovereignty has traditionally been seen as a defining element of state power, and essential for nationhood. It was extolled in the classical works of Hobbes, Locke and Rousseau. But nationalism as a politico-territorial concept didn't stand the test of time though. Rousseau raised a pertinent question contradicting this argument. 'If Sparta and Rome perished, what state can hope to endure forever,' he asked.

Some scholars have added cultural dimension to the definition. Canadian philosopher Michel Seymour gives a 'sociocultural definition' that nation is a cultural group, possibly but not necessarily united by a common descent, endowed with civic ties.

Definitional variations abound. The early German elaborations talk about 'the spirit of a people', while somewhat later ones, mainly of French extraction, talk about 'collective mentality'. Isaiah Berlin, writing as late as in the early 1970s, proposed as a part of his definition of nationalism, that it consists of the conviction that people belong to a particular human group, and that 'the characters of the individuals who compose the group are shaped by, and cannot be understood apart from, those of the group...'

There are some scholars who believed that the concept of nation itself is artificial and imagined. British-Czech philosopher Ernest Gellner observed that nationalism is an 'invention' or fabrication. 'Nationalism is not the awakening of nations to self-consciousness; it invents nations where they do not exist,' he dismissively stated. Benedict Anderson, the Anglo-Irish historian, authored a book claiming that nations were 'imagined communities'.

This insufficient understanding of the concept of nation and nationalism had encouraged the British to proclaim that India was never a nation. Sir John Strachey, a member of the Council of the Secretary of State of the British government, wrote in 1888: 'This is the first and the most essential thing to learn about India that there is not and never was an India or even any country of India possessing, according to European ideas, any sort of unity, physical, political, social or religious. No Indian nation, no people of India of which we hear so much.' The Simon Commission, which came to India in 1928, had referred to India as a 'conglomeration of races and religions.'

Some Indian scholars, too, fell for this European discourse. Surendranath Banerjee, an eminent leader of the Indian National Congress, was prominent among them. Banerjee authored a book titled *A Nation in Making*, in which he observed that India was being made into a nation, thanks largely to the British efforts. At the time of the making of the Constitution of India, both B.R. Ambedkar and Nehru also toed the line that India was to be made into a nation with the help of the new Constitution.

Article 1 of the Constitution of India begins with the statement, 'India, that is Bharat, shall be a Union of States...' Rarely does one come across such a description about nations with two names—one a colonial name and the other, a native one. Independent India couldn't decide upon the question of what identity to give to this nation, primarily because of the confusion in the initial years about whether the newly independent entity was already a nation or a new one under creation. The British had claimed that such an entity came into existence when British India became a member of the League of Nations after World War I.

The Constitution of India borrowed heavily from many constitutions in the world. The very opening sentence of the Preamble to the Constitution, 'We the People of India' was also borrowed from the American constitution, which begins with the statement, 'We the People of the United States.' When the issue came up before the Constituent Assembly of India, many politically-minded members preferred 'We the Indian Nation' in place of 'We the people.' However, Ambedkar opposed the view stating that it was a 'delusion' to think that there was an Indian nation.

Ambedkar held this view right from the time of his dialogues with Gandhi in the 1930s. 'First of all, there is no nation of the Indians in the real sense of the word. The nation does not exist, it is to be created,' he argued. Describing nation as a 'spiritual principle', Ambedkar argued that the Hindus 'lack the consciousness of kind' to be called a nation. What existed in every Hindu was only the 'consciousness of his caste', he bemoaned. His proposition of the making of a nation was based on his view that unless caste divisions are mitigated, the nation in India cannot flourish.

Rabindranath Tagore, too, incidentally, was a strong critic of nation and nationalism. He called nationalism 'a cruel epidemic of evil'. But in India's case, Tagore believed that it 'has all along been trying experiments in evolving a social unity within which all the different peoples could be held together, while fully enjoying the freedom of maintaining their own differences. This has produced something like a United States of a social federation, whose common name is Hinduism.'

Most of these scholars have viewed Indian nationalism from the European prism: According to Indian journalist Girilal Jain:

> The concept of nation itself is, in fact, alien to the Hindu temperament and genius. It is essentially Semitic in character, even if it arose in Western Europe in the eighteenth century when it had successfully shaken off the Church's stranglehold. For, like Christianity and Islam, it too emphasizes the exclusion of those who do not belong to the charmed circle (territorial, or linguistic, or ethnic) as much as it emphasizes the inclusion of those who fall within the circle. Indeed, the former, like the heretics and pagans in Christianity and Islam, are cast into outer darkness.

Sri Aurobindo rejected the Western theory that the essential conditions of nationality are unity of language, unity of religion and life and unity of race. He pointed out that the English nation itself was built out of various races, that Switzerland has distinct racial strains speaking three different languages and professing different religions, that in America, the candidates for White House addressed the nation at one time in fourteen languages, that Austria is a congeries of races and languages. In an illuminating passage, Sri Aurobindo defined the essential elements of nationality:

> [...] there are certain essential conditions—geographical unity, a common past, a powerful common interest impelling towards unity and certain favourable political conditions which enable the impulse to realize itself in an organized government expressing the nationality and perpetuating its single and united existence. A common enthusiasm coalescing with a common interest is the most powerful fosterer of nationality.

Deendayal Upadhyaya argued that when a group of people lives with a goal, an ideal, a mission and looks upon a particular land as motherland, the group constitutes a nation. 'If either of the two—an ideal and a motherland—is not there, then there is no nation,' he observed. Upadhyaya called nation a 'living organism'. It evolves over millennia through historical and civilizational experiences. He explained:

> When a human community living in a certain tract of land for centuries starts experiencing a certain identity with it; customises the special qualities of its life; develops a common set of traditions; a common life mission; common feelings of happiness and sorrow; common experience of friends and foes; a common history through which its great saints and sages nurture that great civilisation through their penance and sacrifice—it is then that a nation with distinct cultural life is born.

In his concept, nation is a spirit, a feeling and an emotion. It is not just about the land, not even about the people. A land and a people together constitute a country. In the West, besides these two prerequisites, a common racial or historical identity was described as the basis for nationhood. But Upadhyaya differentiated between a country, which is a product of land and people coming together through a legal document like a constitution and a government, and a nation which is all of them but much more. He used to cite the example of Israel to raise the important question that for centuries, even when they did not have the land and a united people, much less a government of their own, hadn't the Jewish nation existed?

The Jews lived in many countries as persecuted refugees for centuries. On a specific occasion in a year, the Jewish people used to get together at a place in countries wherever they were living, remember their fatherland, history and ancestors; and while departing, would shake hands with each other with a greeting: 'Next time, in Jerusalem.' This became a mantra for the Jews all over the world for centuries until their cherished Fatherland became a reality in April 1948. Once the new Jewish nation of Israel was born, the Jews from all over the world started pouring into it. They didn't know the land or Hebrew language; they didn't have any knowledge of their customs and traditions; yet, they left everything behind in the countries of living and flocked to the 'Promised Land', almost empty-handed. What was that sentiment that had lived on for centuries even when there was no country or government of their own? What was that sentiment that had motivated them to return to their Fatherland leaving behind their hard-earned wealth and prosperity? That was the sentiment of nationhood. Upadhyaya called it the 'eternal reality'.

Shimon Peres, former Israeli prime minister (PM), in his book *No Room for Small Dreams*, makes an interesting observation about the Jewish nation:

> The Jewish people have lived by the guiding principle of *tikkum olam*—the ambition to improve the whole world, not just ourselves. We lived in exile for two thousand years, without land, without independence, held together not by borders, but by this simple set of values that have echoed

> through history—in Hebrew, in Yiddish, in Ladino—in every language of every country into which the Jewish people dispersed. It is the basis of our identity. And it is from this moral code that we knew, fundamentally, that Israel was not born to rule over other people, that to do so is in profound opposition to our heritage.

The choice of words shouldn't be missed—'set of values', 'identity', 'moral code' and 'heritage'.

To understand the main distinction between the European and Indian understanding of the nation, one can refer to a profound observation made by the eminent Indian author and novelist Raja Rao. 'It is not the Indian who makes India, but India makes the Indian,' he cryptically observed once.

The 'Prince of Paradox', G.K. Chesterton, had once described America as a 'nation with the soul of a church.' The immediate provocation for Chesterton's observation was the questions asked for his entry into America. When he entered the American consulate to secure papers for travelling to America, the application form that he was handed down contained questions like 'Are you an anarchist?', 'Are you a polygamist?', and so on. Irked and amused by these questions, Chesterton started pondering over the traits of the Americans, and the result was an autobiographical book titled *What I Saw in America?*—'America is the only nation in the world that is founded on a creed,' he concludes. Chesterton's observations sparked a major debate in the world. Do nations, like individuals, have souls?

Decades before Chesterton, another great Englishman from Chesterton's country, Benjamin Disraeli, a conservative strongman and the two-time PM of Britain, had championed the idea of national character. 'Nations have characters,' Disraeli insisted.

Psychologists have disagreements over the efforts to find a common characteristic of nations. The so-called national soul or character, to them, appeared over-generalized leading to stereotyping of the nations.

'Germans don't laugh', one stereotype goes, because they are 'sticklers for order to the point of absurdity'. The French are typical playboys always thinking of wine and women. The Americans are fond of expensive cars; the Russians, uncouth, pugnacious and reckless, fond of vodka and street brawls. This kind of trivial stereotyping of nations in the name of national character has led to the manufacturing of several jokes as well. One such joke in Russia goes something like this: what will people of different nationalities do when they see a fly in their glass of beer? The German, being a practical guy, will remove the fly and drink the beer. The Frenchman, being an idealist, will fish out the fly, wipe it, allows it to fly away and discard the beer. The Russian will drink the beer along with the fly, while the American, a conscious guy about his rights, will summon the waiter, scold him to his heart and demand for another glass of beer.

Such stereotyping of the national character is no doubt incorrect. However, to deny that nations have their own character like individuals, and it is reflected in its social mores, customs and traditions, is also equally incorrect.

Two philosophers, Sri Aurobindo from India and Georg Hegel from Germany, had alluded to the concept of national soul in their writings. 'The nation or society, like the individual, has a body, an organic life, a moral and aesthetic temperament, a developing mind and a soul... [I]t is a group soul that, once having attained a distinctness, must then become more and more self-conscious...,' wrote Aurobindo.

Hegel saw 'pure Spirit incarnating into the world, not just as one great beam of light, but as refracted light of many different rays.' He described these rays as incarnating into particular geographical regions that have an ecological integrity or clear boundaries. The local ecology—fauna, flora and humanity—interacts with the incoming ray of spirit, and the result of that interaction eventually becomes a nation. Hegel then goes on to talk about a soul for each such nation. He called it the 'volksgeist', or folk soul. 'The national folk soul, which has also been described as an over-lighting angel, carries the unique energy of its people and can be seen manifesting in the culture, songs and myths of its people. This loose-knit grouping of peoples eventually unifies as the Spirit of the nascent nation incarnates more fully,' Hegel argued. To put it simply, Hegel believed that nation was nothing but a spirit with a folk soul, which manifests through the culture, myths, and at a sophisticated level, even in the form of the state.

Deendayal Upadhyaya used the word *'chiti'* for describing the national soul. Every nation has its own chiti. He wrote:

> Chiti is fundamental and is central to the nation from its very beginning. Chiti determines the direction in which the nation is to advance culturally. Whatever is in accordance with chiti is included in culture. Chiti is the touchstone on which each action, each attitude is tested, and determined to be acceptable or otherwise. Chiti is the soul of the nation. It is on the foundation of this chiti that a nation arises and becomes strong and virile.

The first PM of India, Jawaharlal Nehru, was a modernist seeped in Western ideological traditions. Yet, he too invoked this concept of the national soul in his famous 'Tryst with Destiny' address to Parliament at midnight on 14 August 1947 when India became independent. He said:

> Long years ago, we made a tryst with destiny, and now the time comes when we shall redeem our pledge, not wholly or in full measure, but very substantially. At the stroke of the midnight hour, when the world sleeps, India will awake to life and freedom. A moment comes, which comes but rarely in history, when we step out from the old to the new, when an age ends, and when the soul of a nation, long suppressed, finds utterance.

The Indian word for denoting this eternal emotional and spiritual idea of nationhood, as distinct from the European racial, political and geographical idea of the nation, is '*rashtram*'. Rashtram is the Indian concept of nationhood. Rashtram is a living organism manifested through a national soul. Rashtram is the alter-nationalism of Tagore and Ram Rajya of Gandhi.

References to rashtram can be found in many places in ancient Indian literature. In Rig Veda, rashtram was used to describe the national identity of the people of the land called Bharatavarsha. Rashtram as an idea is a unifying and development-oriented (*abhyudayam*) concept as against today's concept of nation, in which the basic urge to live together in harmony is not developed, and which has been a major source of political conflict and violence throughout the history of the last several centuries.

Rashtram has been invested with divinity and motherhood in the Vedas. Sage Vac, one of the many women composers of the hymns in the Vedas, says in the tenth mandala of the Rig Veda, '*Aham Rashtri Sangamani Vasunam Chikitushi Prathama Yagyiyanam* (I am the beholder of this rashtra; benefactor of the gods; and first among the worshipped)'.

Thus, an effort was made to infuse the sense of divinity, sacredness and motherhood in rashtram from the Rig Vedic times. Nation is a feminine entity in India as against the common Western masculine understanding of the Fatherland. This Vedic hymn is in a sense the origin of the concept of Bharat Mata—the Motherland Bharat. Sri Aurobindo described her as '*Jagajjanani*'—the mother of all mothers—the Universal Mother.

In the foreword to R.K. Mookerji's *The Fundamental Unity of India*, Ramsay MacDonald, former PM of Britain writes:

> The Hindu regards India not only as a political unit naturally the subject of one sovereignty—whoever holds that sovereignty, whether British, Mohammedan, or Hindu—but as the outward embodiment, as the temple—nay, even as the goddess mother—of his spiritual culture… He made India the symbol of his culture; he filled it with this soul. In his consciousness, it was his greater self.

This distinct idea of nation as rashtram evolved in India through the efforts of countless saints and sages, who deliberated upon the mission of the nation and came up with the concept of *bhadra iccha* (benign wish). The Atharva Veda states that the rashtram—the national identity of the people of India—was the product of that bhadra iccha of those sages.

Bhadram icchhantah rishiyah
swar vidayah, tapo dikshaamupanshed agre.
tato raashtram, bala, ojasya jaatam
tadasmai devaupasannmantu

It means that a bhadra icchha had originated in the minds of ancient seers during the course of their penance. This benign wish was for abhyudayam—the welfare and glory of all. This is not divisive and is not guided by any selfish desire for personal pleasures.

In order to fulfil the bhadra icchha for abhyudayam, a doctrine of dharma, set of moral codes, was developed. Sage

Kanada in Vaisesika Sutra defines dharma by its beneficial impact: '*Yatobhyudaya nisreyasa siddhihi ca dharmah* (That which leads to the attainment of abhyudaya [material prosperity in this world] and nihsreyasa [total cessation of pain and attainment of eternal bliss hereafter] is dharma).' The bhadra icchha of the sages was to secure this two-fold objective.

Dharma manifests in the chiti—national soul of India as a rashtram. It includes the outlook to life, creation, universe, god, state, wealth and everything else. It is these ideals on which the Indian nationhood—*rashtriyata*—was founded and thrived. It is these ideals that India has 'never lost sight of' in her long journey through victories and vicissitudes.

The moral and ethical value system that is described as dharma is a product of the Indian genius evolved over millennia of the penance and dialogue of its sages and saints. It is universal. In fact, the Hindus call it Sanatana Dharma—an eternal value system, universal in time and space. In the course of a long history, the sages and saints of India have defined the concept of dharma variously.

In the Shanti Parva of the Mahabharata, it was stated: '*Yah syatprabhavasamyuktah sa dharma iti nischayah* (That which is able to bring about evolution is called dharma)'.

Adi Shankara described dharma as: '*Jagatah Sthitikaranam Praninam Sakshat Abhyudaya Nishreyasa Heturyah sa Dharmah* (Dharma is that which accomplishes exceptional administration of the entire world, brings about the worldly progress of every living being and causes progress in the spiritual realm as well)'.

'*Dharmasaram Idam Jagat* (This entire universe is the essence of Dharma),' proclaims sage Valmiki in the 'Aranya Kanda' of the Ramayana.

Dharma as a view of life goes about enumerating a set of moral and ethical values for mankind. It is these values that delineate the ethical foundation of Indian nationhood.

As mentioned in the Isavasya Upanishad, on the question of Creation, the Dharmic worldview believes: '*Isavasyam idam sarvam* (The entire universe, animate and inanimate alike, is pervaded by Isvara, the divine consciousness)'.

This concept of the omnipresence of divinity must be understood in the face of the confusion arising out of the Christian doctrines of monotheism and polytheism. The Indian Dharmic worldview is neither. It can at best be described as 'omnitheism'.

The Christian worldview attributes divinity only to the Trinity—The Father, the Son and the Holy Spirit, whereas the Dharmic worldview sees divinity everywhere. When divinity is omnipresent, why must there be conflicts over religion, race, caste and nationality? The Hindu answer is the pervasive *maya* (illusion).

On the question of ethnic, racial, linguistic and other difference in the world, the Dharmic worldview proposes '*Vasudhaiva Kutumbakam* (The entire world as one family)'.

The West, in the name of globalization, talked about global markets. The Dharmic worldview talks about a global family. The daily prayer of an aged, illiterate and poor village woman in a corner or India starts with *Ganga Mata ki Jai* (Victory to Mother Ganges) and ends with *Lok Kalyan Ho* (Glory to the Entire World).

On the economic question, it talks about 'sustained consumption'—'*Tena tyaktena bhunjitah* (One should acquire only that much which was left for him by Isvara)'.

After traversing through many economic theories, the West is now coming round to the view that for achieving sustainable development, we need to advocate for sustainable consumption also.

On the welfare question, it states, '*Sarve bhavantu sukinah, Sarve santu niramayah* (Let all be happy and free from diseases)'.

This is in contrast to the West's theory of maximum benefit to the maximum number.

As mentioned in the Atharva Veda, in the environment-related questions, its proposition is, '*Mata bhumih putro'ham prithvyah* (This earth is my mother, and I am her son)'.

Worship of nature is against the core Western idea of the exploitation of nature. From Socrates and Plato downwards, it was believed that man should master nature, whereas the Dharmic worldview insisted that it should be worshipped as mother and only 'milked' like a child does from its mother, not exploited.

On the question of religious diversity in the world, the Dharmic worldview proposes, '*Ekam Sadvipraa bahudhaa Vadanti maatarisvaanamaahuh* (Truth is one; wise men interpret in different ways)'.

The Dharmic worldview stands for pluralism and diversity. It abhors uniformity and rejection. Contrary to the Semitic worldview which insisted about the possession of the 'ultimate reality', the dharmic worldview suggested that the 'ultimate reality' is an endless search by man. Gandhi called the Sanatana Dharma as an 'endless search for truth'.

The ethical and spiritual nationhood of India is a benign and universal idea. It sustained India's unity as a nation for millennia. Like all path-breaking ideas, this nationhood also faces certain contemporary challenges.

India's national consciousness was jolted into action when it came face-to-face with the Semitic worldview. The exclusivist Islamic concept of Ummah—a supra-national community of Muslims—posed the first ever serious challenge to the rashtram. India had to endure a Partition as a consequence. The two-nation theory of Jinnah was a complete anti-thesis of the inclusive concept of national consciousness in India. There are forces to this day in India that believe in that theory.

The other challenge is the possible Semitization of Indic thought, where Indian society, as a reaction to Semitic exclusivism, starts internalizing those very exclusivist mores.

The forces of Partition were actively supported by the Indian communists who argued that India was not a single nation but a conglomeration of 16 different nationalities. The heady cocktail of these two forces of separatism and exclusivism can be witnessed in prestigious academic institutions even now. The Tukde Tukde gangs whose slogan is '*Bharat, tere tukde honge* (India, you will be broken down into pieces)' are still active.

False application of the notion of secularism, an essentially European concept, is another serious challenge. Much before secularism came into vogue in Europe, India practised the idea of *Sarva Panth Samaadar* (equal respect for all religions). K.T. Shah, a member of the Constituent Assembly, wanted the word 'secular' to be explicitly stated in the Constitution. But both Nehru and Ambedkar didn't seem inclined. All members agreed that secularism should be respected. But which secularism? Is it the European understanding of separation of the church and state or the American understanding of freedom of religion? Nehru viewed the Indian nation as cultural and Ambedkar viewed it as spiritual. Both believed that the Western secularist concept will lead to confusion. Hence, the Constitution of India did not contain the word 'secular' until 1976.

The flawed secularism discourse in India tries to negate the moral and ethical value system by using an erroneous concept of dharma *Nirapekshata*. Translated into English, it means 'non-relation to religion'. Confusion stems from the use of the word 'Dharma', whereas the correct word for religion should be 'panth'. India's national motto is, as inscribed on the national symbol, the Ashok Chakra, '*Dharma Chakra Pravartanaya*'—meaning, 'the wheels of Dharma should keep on rolling'.

While in the West the state has been identified with the nation, in Indian national consciousness, the state is never regarded as a superior institution. Devotion to king is not warranted; instead, devotion to nation is promoted. Talking about the relationship between the nation and the state, Upadhyaya says:

> Self-rule is only useful and effective until the point that it fulfils the requirements of the motherland. This can only happen when the national society progresses from the worship of the state to the worship of the nation. True capability lies not in the state, but in the nation. The nation is the sole truth. Devotion to this truth has been described as a cultural duty. Political duties can only be successful when these intensive national values are bolstered by the strength of cultural duties that accompany them.

In the long history, India was rarely ruled by one sovereign ruler. Events like Rajasuya would occasionally give rise to emperors with suzerainty over their subjects, but never a single state. The *Aitareya Brahmana*, one of the ancient texts of India, describes 10 kinds of *rajya*s under one *rashtra*: *samrajyam. bhaujyam. svarajyam. vairajyam. parameshthyam. rajyam. maharajyam adhipatyamayam. samantaparyay syat. sarvabhauma sarvayusha.*

There were autocratic monarchs, hereditary kings and democratic republics living side-by-side. There were instances when foreign aggressors had occupied some of these states and established kingdoms. Greek conquerors like Alexander and Seleucus came, Huns, Shakas and Kushans came. They established their kingdoms for some time over parts of the territory of this country. Then came the Islamic hordes. Muhammad bin Qasim was the first Islamic invader to occupy the Sindh province in today's Pakistan in the early eighth century. From then, to the eighteenth century, many parts of the Indian nation were under Muslim rule. After that came the British who ruled over almost the entire Indian territory for two centuries. During all this time, the state was under alien control. Yet, the nation didn't cease to exist. The soul of this nation existed elsewhere, in its religions, culture, pilgrimages, social institutions and many other entities.

In fact, the state as a political institution was even seen as dispensable. In Mahabharata, there comes a narrative about the first epoch of the Hindu almanac, the Krita Yuga. The relevant verse reads like this—'*Na Rajyam Naiva Rajasit Na Dando na ca Dandikaha / Dharmenaiva Praja Sarvaha Rakshantisma Parasparam* (There was no state; no king. There was none to be punished and none to punish. People have protected each other through the eternal principles of Dharma)'.

Thus, aeons before Marx envisaged 'withering away of the state', the Indian nation had experienced such a state of statelessness. Yet, the national life continued on the basis of dharma.

Chanakya states that the rajah is a servant of dharma. Unlike in nation states, the rajah enjoys no special privileges whatsoever. He is mandated to live like a commoner. The happiness of the rajah lies in the happiness of his subjects. Even his powers as a ruler are subject to the scrutiny of dharma. When a rajah is coronated, he would declare thrice that he is above punishment. A revered sage is then made to pronounce thrice '*Dharmadandyosi* (Dharma will punish you)'.

The challenge is when the state assumes all-encompassing powers and all other civic institutions become subservient to it. Loyalty to the state then becomes the sine qua non of nationalism.

The ancient nationhood of India withstood many such vicissitudes and challenges. Nevertheless, India needs to be vigilant about these challenges because it has, as Vivekananda put it, 'a destiny to fulfil, duty to perform and mission to accomplish'. That mission is not just local or national. It is global and beyond.

Sri Aurobindo described the Indian approach to the eternal nature of Indian nationalism in the following words:

> In India we do not recognise the nation as the highest synthesis to which we can rise. There is a higher synthesis, humanity; beyond that there is a still higher synthesis, this living, suffering, aspiring world of creatures, the synthesis of Buddhism; there is a highest of all, the synthesis of God, and that is the Hindu synthesis, the synthesis of Vedanta. With us today nationalism is our immediate practical faith and gospel not because it is the highest possible synthesis, but because it must be realised in life. We must live as a nation before we can live in humanity.

Reprinted from OPEN MAGAZINE, with permission of Open Media Network Pvt. Ltd.

Index